Beyond the Algorithm: Human-Centered Systems for AI, Learning, and Global Trust

By: Michael Torrence, Ph.D.

Acknowledgments

To my wife Jamie Torrence, Ph.D., for providing me space to dream and explore, all the while encouraging me to remain a curious and insatiable learner … I am boundlessly grateful. To my daughter Anna, for walking through the world with joy coupled with unfettered strength and an explorer's heart and my son Jack, for participating in and observing all around you with quiet strength and wise discernment. To both of you, the world awaits your continued contributions and bright lion-like voices of civility, common sense, and humor. To my son Jake, protector, keep the main thing the focal point of your resolve and drive your intentions forward without breaks because society needs and hungers for integrity and character … to all my children, LEAD!!!! To my mother, Janet Torrence, thank you for wisdom and grace, patience and resolve, intention and purpose … the Sun is in the design. To Alissa and Brenda, we can do all things and thank you both for simply being and choosing to be a part of the journey … To the inner circle, those who know and need no names, let's keep our eyes and ears open, our hands free, and our mouths prepared to articulate and endeavour on behalf of each other's growth and being reminded that trust is in the truth. We remain peppered across the globe and linked like chains navigating our halls, institutions, chambers, wards, and communities like old samurai and griots. Tell the story, share the story, and live the story. It has all been written. To those who will read these words, thank you for your time, reflection, and engaging with me sweeping into your consciousness. Let's GO!

-MT/2025

Table of Contents

Prologue: Out in Front & Leading While Doing

Leadership has always carried with it a paradox: one must both chart the course and walk it. The most durable leaders are not those who lead from behind glass or from a podium alone, but those who stand out in front-visible, accountable, and committed to the labor of doing as much as to the art of directing. To lead while doing is not merely symbolic; it is the praxis of credibility. It is the daily act of demonstrating that the future we speak into existence is one we are willing to test, refine, and sometimes stumble through in real time.

In this era of artificial intelligence, educational technology, shifting policies, and evolving governance, the necessity of leading while doing has never been clearer. We live in a time when algorithms mediate decisions once made by human deliberation, when credentials are exchanged as digital assets rather than parchment, and when institutions of learning are asked to prove their value not only in classrooms, but in economic mobility, workforce resilience, and ethical stewardship. The promise and peril of AI forces leaders to be translators, conduits, interpreters, and bridge-builders between technical sophistication and human aspiration.

This prologue is not a proclamation of answers, but an invitation to witness the messy, necessary work of applied leadership. The work is iterative: to test an AI model for student success is to wrestle with equity, governance, and data integrity. To champion policy that accelerates technological adoption is to simultaneously safeguard the human dignity of those the policies affect. To teach in the digital age is to learn anew every day what it means to listen, to adapt, and to create meaning beyond the confines of the algorithm. The further we code and create, the closer we must become as a society of learners and agents of opportunity.

To be out in front is to endure the risks of visibility, but also to embrace the privilege of shaping what comes next. As we move deeper into the post-algorithmic age, my aim is not only to analyze the technologies that shape us, but also to model how leaders can embody a practice of guided autonomy: where vision and execution converge, where bold imagination is matched with disciplined stewardship, and where leadership is never divorced from the act of doing.

This book continues that journey. It carries forward the work of imagining futures, questioning assumptions, and building systems of trust in a world defined by velocity, instances, uncertainty, and potential. To those who read these words-students, educators, industry and business partners, policymakers, innovators-I extend both a challenge and a promise: let us not wait for the future to arrive passively. Let us lead while doing, out in front, together.

Chapter 1 - From Transformation to Stewardship: The Evolution of AI Discourse

We ended our last conversation with a promise - not to ourselves alone, but to the generations who will inherit the systems we design. We spoke of planting trees for which we may never sit under, of committing to shade and shelter we may never personally enjoy. That is not sentimentality. That is a fort on the River Lune. That is a Lancaster. That is honest. That is stewardship.

Volume I was about transformation - the hard work of building, testing, and iterating. We wrestled with AI's place in learning, the redesign of workforce pipelines, the moral questions around digital access, and the proof-of-concept for systems like Metaversity and universally integrated credential systems. We made the case for inclusion as an imperative, not an afterthought. Moreover, we advanced a local-to-national model for linking learning to earning.

Now, the scaffolding we built is no longer ours alone. Others - nations, industries, communities far beyond Tennessee - are climbing it, modifying it, and using it as the launch platform for their own AI-enabled futures. The question is no longer can we build it? We can, and we have. The questions before us now are: how will we maintain it, govern it, and evolve it so it remains trustworthy, equitable, and adaptive in a world that is both local and planetary?

This is the shift from transformation to stewardship ... In an age of accelerated interdependence, stewardship becomes increasingly crucial. In the early years of AI integration, much of the public discourse was about novelty: could AI teach, diagnose, predict, optimize? Those were important questions, but they were also shallow waters. They allowed us to admire the technology without confronting the responsibilities that come with wielding it. How broad of a tool can AI be? What can the tool shoulder and will it be useful and not just used.

Today, AI is not simply a tool in our classrooms, boardrooms, or laboratories. It is in our networks, in our supply chains, in our medical imaging, and in our disaster response systems. It is designing with us, and in some cases, designing for us. AI is co-thinking, co-building, co-experimenting, co-collaborating, and absolutely drawing on the emotions of those who would call it cohabitator. That is why stewardship is not optional. Without intentional governance and collaborative oversight, AI will drift toward the interests of those most able to exploit it, rather than those most in need of its benefits.

Stewardship requires that we move beyond technical literacy to ethical fluency - the ability to navigate questions of bias, sovereignty, and shared ownership with the same rigor we apply to algorithms and data models. This is the opportunity to spark imitative and robust mock ups and diagrams for those who will serve as carriers of what humanism will extend to and become. We will start from local models and mature into global trust. Our work in Tennessee - in community colleges, with industry partners, and in coalition with state agencies - was never meant to be a self-contained experiment. It was designed to be transformative and transferable: an interoperable way of leaking and linking learning → credentialing → employment that could be mirrored in any geography, adapted to local cultures and economies. We want to dare boldly that what we create is beautiful beyond the aesthetics of a mirror. What we create is interoperable.

The stewardship lens forces us to ask:

1. What does trust look like when the network is not just local or national, but intercontinental?

2. Who holds the keys to identity verification when credentials cross borders?

3. How do we maintain privacy in a world of real-time data exchange between sovereign nations?

4. Can a small rural learning system plug into a global AI network without being subsumed by it?

Trust, in this sense, is not simply a matter of compliance or certification. It is a living network. A network of networks - that grows stronger the more transparently it operates, the more agency it returns to individuals, and the more it honors cultural context. What is trustworthy is not fed untruths, agreed?

A New Measure of Success

In Volume I, our benchmarks for success included enrollment, completion, credential attainment, and workforce placement. In stewardship, those are still necessary, but insufficient. A future-proof measure of success must also ask:

1. Are systems interoperable across sectors and borders?

2. Are credentials recognized without diluting local relevance? Is the data lifecycle ethical, transparent, and secure?

3. Do emerging technologies (humanoids, quantum computing, spatial systems, and others) enhance equity or exacerbate divides?

These are not abstract questions. These are not expressionist abstractions of Pollockian drip. They are design constraints for the next decade. If we fail to address them now, we will find ourselves retrofitting ethics and trust into systems that have already calcified - a costly and often impossible task. Musings aside, we fortify.

Stewardship is a Global Commons. Stewardship demands coalition. No single institution, company, or government can hold the line on equity, access, and safety alone. That is why the next chapters will focus on universally integrated systems, trust networks, and coalitions that count - models where public, private, and civic actors share responsibility for the commons we are building.

The commons of the 21st century is not just air, water, and land. It is data, algorithms, and the interoperability of our learning and innovation systems. And just as environmental stewardship asks us to consider the next hundred years, so too must AI stewardship require long-horizon thinking. We must sustain, adapt, and advance.

The following are areas I hope to explore at some later date or that others may have already begun to explore. Ownership of questions and subsequent solutions escape me, the academician seeks to learn, to know, to embody, and this method of yearning for learning and its implicative impacts drives parts of us. When pontificating on the following themes; democratic participation, interdependence and responsibility, knowledge and power, time and change, values in translation, failure and recovery, I land here with these representations seeking responsive dialogue and more than answers ...

When we build governance structures that can adapt quickly enough to remain relevant, can we do so while being stable enough to provide meaningful oversight of those who will be bound to the frameworks, guidelines, and parameters that we set and how flexible we might need to be due to the accelerated pace of AI advancement? Perhaps this attempt at guidance for government principles provides timely observations or salient points. We know that AI is not a bazooka to be shot at everything, but where it can move our efforts.

AI governance must begin with an uncompromising focus on mission. In higher education, this mission is centered on advancing student success, enabling workforce mobility, and stewarding public trust. When institutions adopt AI without grounding in mission, they risk investing in tools that distract from core priorities, duplicate existing systems, or introduce risks that outweigh benefits. A mission-first lens serves as a filter, ensuring AI is not pursued for novelty or efficiency alone but because it measurably advances institutional goals. This principle also builds consistency across decision-making: when a mission serves as the anchor, stakeholders understand both why an AI initiative is launched and why another is declined.

Embedding mission alignment into AI governance aligns with frameworks like the U.S. Department of Education's Office of Educational Technology, which emphasizes that technology integration should be leveraged to expand equity, quality, and lifelong learning opportunities (tech.ed.gov). It forces institutions to ask: Will this tool improve learning outcomes, reduce inequity, or strengthen workforce preparation? If the answer is not demonstrably "yes," governance should pause the deployment. Such disciplined alignment provides a defensible narrative for both internal and external audiences.

Finally, mission alignment protects institutional credibility. Faculty, students, parents, regulators, and community partners are more likely to trust AI initiatives when their relevance to mission is clear and transparent. Governance councils can codify this by requiring an explicit "mission statement" for every AI project before approval. This not only disciplines decision-making but also signals institutional integrity-showing that AI is not a passing fad but a carefully stewarded tool for advancing collective purpose.

Governance systems collapse when they either overburden low-risk innovation or under-scrutinize high-impact decisions. Proportionality ensures that AI oversight scales with the level of consequence rather than applying a blanket compliance framework to all systems. In practice, this means that a course-planning chatbot can move through a "green lane" with lighter checks, while an AI that informs hiring or grading decisions must undergo rigorous testing, external review, and continuous monitoring. Proportionality balances innovation and accountability, preserving institutional agility while upholding responsibility in areas where harm could be significant.

This principle is mirrored in the National Institute of Standards and Technology's (NIST) AI Risk Management Framework, which provides a scalable approach to identifying, measuring, and managing risks across contexts (nist.gov). Rather than creating one rulebook for all AI, NIST advocates tailoring controls to the type of harm, likelihood, and affected population. For higher education and workforce systems, proportionality prevents resource misallocation: faculty tools that are low-risk are not delayed, while critical systems like financial aid, advising, or admissions receive priority oversight.

Proportionality also helps cultivate a culture of trust and engagement among faculty, staff, and students. If low-risk tools face the same barriers as high-risk ones, stakeholders may perceive governance as bureaucratic obstruction rather than stewardship. Conversely, clear tiering reassures stakeholders that high-stakes applications will receive the attention they deserve. By embedding proportionality into governance policy, institutions create structures that are both stable and adaptable-stable in principle, adaptive in application.

Complex AI systems do not fail in linear ways; they fail across technical, human, and organizational boundaries. Defense-in-depth acknowledges this by embedding overlapping safeguards that together build resilience. At the technical level, this might include automated model testing and bias detection. At the human level, it requires oversight committees, red-team reviews, and clearly documented escalation paths. Organizationally, it requires policies, cultural norms, and reporting mechanisms that anticipate mistakes. Each layer is designed to catch what the other misses, creating a safety net that prevents small oversights from becoming systemic failures.

The U.S. Government Accountability Office (GAO) emphasizes the importance of layered oversight in its AI accountability framework, noting that no single control is sufficient to address the complexity of AI risks (gao.gov). Defense-in-depth ensures redundancy is viewed not as inefficiency but as resilience. For instance, even if an automated system passes technical testing, a human reviewer may catch errors invisible to the algorithm. In this way, institutions avoid over-reliance on any one safeguard, recognizing that true safety emerges from the interplay of multiple protective layers.

Embedding defense-in-depth also creates institutional readiness. When an incident does occur, a culture of layered oversight allows for quicker detection, clearer accountability, and faster recovery. By structuring safeguards across multiple levels, institutions can better assure regulators, funders, and communities that they are serious about stewardship. Defense-in-depth moves governance from a reactive posture to a proactive stance, embodying resilience as a core value. No AI, however advanced, should make high-stakes decisions autonomously.

Human-in-command ensures accountability, dignity, and fairness remain central-particularly critical when decisions affect academic outcomes, employment, or access. This principle upholds that AI augments, not replaces, human judgment. For example, an AI might suggest grading rubrics or recommend hiring pools, but humans must review, interpret context, and hold authority for final action.

U.S. frameworks like the AI Bill of Rights emphasize the right to human alternatives and fallback-mandating that individuals have access to human attention when decisions impact them significantly (whitehouse.gov). In practice, AI systems must include override mechanisms, appeal routes, and transparency about when automation influenced outcomes. This supports ethical stewardship and protects against dehumanization, preserving institutional legitimacy and human values.

Human-in-command also has pedagogical implications. In higher education, faculty should always remain the ultimate arbiters of grading and assessment, even if AI supports feedback or content evaluation. Similarly, in workforce credentialing, human oversight prevents unfair exclusions and ensures appeals processes are accessible. Governance structures that enshrine human-in-command provide both technical assurance and moral reassurance, strengthening institutional trust.

True transparency isn't a dump of technical specs; it's meaningful communication tailored to stakeholder needs. Students need clarity to understand how AI influences advising, grading, or administrative decisions. Faculty need deeper access to documentation of system logic, assumptions, and known limitations. Accreditation and regulatory bodies require evidence linking AI practices to mission compliance.
Transparency with purpose is about matching the right level of disclosure to the right audience.

The University of Arizona emphasizes labeling AI-assisted materials and disclosing usage in educational settings as a best practice for governance (arizona.edu). Such measures ensure that stakeholders are informed without being overwhelmed by technical detail. Transparency builds informed consent, encourages accountability, and prevents the perception that institutions are hiding behind black-box algorithms.

Purposeful transparency also supports community trust beyond the campus.

Local employers, workforce boards, and legislators will expect institutions to articulate clearly how AI supports teaching, training, and workforce development. By establishing communication norms that are honest, accessible, and actionable, institutions strengthen their reputation as trustworthy stewards of emerging technologies.

AI governance must treat privacy not as an add-on but as a core architectural requirement. Privacy-by-design ensures that protections are embedded in every stage-from data collection and storage to model training and deployment. Data minimization complements this by ensuring institutions only collect, store, and process what is absolutely necessary for the intended purpose. Together, these practices reduce exposure to risk, prevent unnecessary data hoarding, and support compliance with regulatory standards.

North Carolina's Department of Information Technology highlights privacy's central role in AI governance, emphasizing that systems should be designed with Fair Information Practice Principles at their core (it.nc.gov). Embedding these practices from the outset ensures institutions are not scrambling to retrofit protections after breaches or legal challenges. It also reinforces ethical obligations to students and employees, many of whom entrust sensitive personal information to institutional systems.

Finally, privacy-by-design supports public trust. In an era of increasing skepticism about data practices, institutions that proactively protect data rights stand apart as leaders in ethical governance. By articulating clear policies and demonstrating real practices, governance structures can transform privacy from a compliance checkbox into a differentiator of institutional integrity.

AI systems will not automatically deliver equity; they often replicate or amplify existing inequalities unless deliberately countered. Equity-by-design embeds fairness as a requirement at every stage of the AI lifecycle. It requires proactive analysis for disparate impacts across demographic groups, corrective measures such as reweighting datasets, and continuous monitoring after deployment. This ensures equity is not an afterthought but a core evaluative standard.

Georgia's statewide AI guidance calls for addressing algorithmic bias through intentional data curation, fairness assessments, and transparent reporting (ai.georgia.gov). For higher education, this means ensuring that advising systems do not disadvantage first-generation students, financial aid models do not exclude vulnerable populations, and workforce placement tools do not systematically filter out underrepresented groups. Equity-by-design operationalizes fairness in measurable ways.

Institutions that take equity seriously gain more than compliance-they build legitimacy. Students, faculty, and community members are more likely to trust AI systems when they can see fairness considerations explicitly addressed. Governance frameworks that elevate equity signal that technological innovation will not come at the expense of justice, but will serve as a lever for greater inclusivity.

Governance without evidence is hollow. Auditability ensures AI systems produce traceable records: what data were used, which models were deployed, which parameters were active, and how outputs were generated. Reproducibility guarantees that decisions can be recreated under the same conditions, allowing institutions to understand, explain, and defend outcomes. These practices provide the foundation for accountability and continuous improvement.

Stanford University's AI guidelines emphasize that even when AI is used to assist, humans remain responsible for outputs and must ensure accountability is maintained (stanford.edu). Institutions must therefore create robust audit trails, including version control of models and data, as well as system cards and assurance cases. This enables governance bodies to review, regulators to inspect, and stakeholders to challenge outcomes when necessary.

Auditability and reproducibility also prepare institutions for the inevitable: errors, challenges, and external scrutiny. By embedding audit mechanisms proactively, institutions demonstrate readiness to face questions transparently. This shifts perception from defensiveness to responsibility, strengthening the institution's position as a trustworthy steward of technology.

AI governance must be dynamic. Static rulebooks quickly become obsolete in a domain defined by rapid technological change. Continuous improvement embeds adaptation into governance through feedback loops: quarterly reviews of risk appetite, post-incident reviews, updates to oversight practices, and adjustments to risk tiering. This ensures governance remains relevant and resilient in changing contexts.

The U.S. General Services Administration (GSA) promotes

"performance-driven governance," encouraging institutions to adapt oversight mechanisms based on real system performance and evolving mission demands (coe.gsa.gov). Embedding learning cycles means that institutions are not locked into outdated practices but remain agile in the face of new risks and opportunities. This turns governance into a living system-one that grows stronger through experience.

Continuous improvement also builds stakeholder confidence. Students, faculty, and employers are more likely to trust governance systems that show evidence of learning, iteration, and growth. By making adaptation a visible and intentional practice, institutions reinforce the message that governance is not about static compliance but about ongoing stewardship. Governance frameworks fail if they lack enforceability. Accountability with teeth ensures that policies are not just aspirational but binding. It requires naming responsible individuals and offices, creating escalation procedures, and defining meaningful consequences for violations. This transforms governance from suggestion into authority.

The Department of Homeland Security's AI principles stress that governance must include accountability structures, where responsibility is clear and consequences are real (dhs.gov). Institutions must adopt a similar approach by assigning system owners, conducting regular reviews, and implementing remediation processes for noncompliance. Without enforceable accountability, governance risks becoming symbolic rather than substantive.

Accountability also protects institutional legitimacy. Students and employees want assurance that someone is answerable if an AI system fails or causes harm. By embedding accountability mechanisms, governance structures demonstrate seriousness and integrity-sending a clear signal that AI stewardship carries weight, responsibility, and consequence.

References - Chapter 1

1. U.S. Department of Education, Office of Educational Technology. Advancing Equity and Opportunity with EdTech. tech.ed.gov

2. National Institute of Standards and Technology (NIST). AI Risk Management Framework. nist.gov

3. U.S. Government Accountability Office. Artificial Intelligence: An Accountability Framework. gao.gov

4. The White House, OSTP. Blueprint for an AI Bill of Rights. whitehouse.gov

5. University of Arizona. Best Practices for AI Governance. infosci.arizona.edu

6. North Carolina Department of Information Technology. Privacy's Role in AI Governance. it.nc.gov

7. State of Georgia. Guidelines for State Organizations on AI. ai.georgia.gov

8. Stanford University. Stanford Principles for AI Use. stanford.edu

9. U.S. General Services Administration, Centers of Excellence. AI Guide for Government: Responsible Implementation. coe.gsa.gov

10. U.S. Department of Homeland Security. Ensuring AI is Used Responsibly. dhs.gov

Chapter 2 - Obligations we have to communities who did not choose to climb it, but are indeed affected by AI

When we introduce transformative technologies such as artificial intelligence, our first responsibility is to those who never volunteered to be early adopters but who nonetheless experience its ripple effects. The communities that did not choose the climb-rural families, underrepresented learners, displaced workers-still live in its shadow. The obligation of mission-first alignment is to ensure that AI is not merely deployed for efficiency or prestige but is anchored in advancing equity, opportunity, and dignity. The U.S. Department of Education underscores that EdTech adoption should serve as a pathway to access, not exclusion (tech.ed.gov). Mission-first alignment insists we ask, who benefits, and who is burdened? And if the burdens fall disproportionately on those without voice, our ethical imperative is to recalibrate until technology advances the common good.

The second obligation lies in proportionality and equity. Communities carry different levels of risk when new systems are introduced without consultation. Marginalized populations often face outsized harm-through biased admissions algorithms, opaque credentialing systems, or workforce transitions that strip opportunity without offering retraining. Here, proportionality demands that we apply the strictest oversight where harm is greatest. Equity-by-design insists that safeguards are woven in from the beginning, not bolted on after damage has occurred. And defense-in-depth ensures there are multiple layers of protection-policy, technical safeguards, human oversight, and cultural norms-that together anticipate harm before it materializes. Georgia's statewide AI guidance makes this obligation explicit: institutions must design systems that mitigate inequities at their root (ai.georgia.gov). For those who never chose the climb, layered protections become a moral covenant of care.

Finally, obligations to affected communities require accountability that is binding, not symbolic. Governance must have teeth-naming responsible actors, requiring evidence of compliance, and imposing real consequences when harms occur.

Continuous improvement adds the humility that governance cannot be static. Feedback from those impacted, even when indirect, must reshape oversight practices over time. The U.S. General Services Administration emphasizes adaptive, performance-driven governance, reminding us that stewardship is an evolving responsibility (coe.gsa.gov). To communities that never chose this climb, our accountability is not optional; it is central to institutional legitimacy.

They deserve the assurance that those who did choose to innovate are carrying the full weight of responsibility-ensuring that progress does not bypass justice, and that the benefits of innovation do not come at the expense of the unheard. We are in a stage where we must consider who must learn AI?

The obligation to determine who must learn AI begins with clarity of mission. In education and workforce contexts, the answer cannot be narrowed to specialists or technologists alone. AI has already woven itself into the daily lives of students, faculty, staff, employers, and communities-even those who may not see themselves as technologists. Thus, mission-first alignment calls us to broaden the frame: AI literacy is not optional for a select few, but foundational for the many. The U.S. Department of Education highlights the importance of digital literacy and AI understanding as essential to preparing learners for a rapidly changing world (tech.ed.gov). By anchoring AI education to institutional missions of access, equity, and mobility, we ensure that the question of "who must learn AI" is answered inclusively. Everyone touched by AI-directly or indirectly-becomes part of the learning obligation.

Still, proportionality demands that not all learners engage at the same depth. For some, AI competency will mean basic fluency-understanding how AI tools shape decisions, what their limitations are, and how to exercise agency. For others-engineers, data scientists, or policymakers-AI learning will be advanced, involving technical mastery, ethical analysis, and governance stewardship.

Equity-by-design insists that AI literacy is not a privilege afforded only to elite institutions or affluent communities; it must be distributed fairly across rural, urban, and marginalized populations. Defense-in-depth ensures that curricula, teacher training, and policy safeguards reinforce one another, so that learners at every level have layered access and protection. The National Science Foundation (NSF) has called for democratizing AI education, underscoring that broad AI literacy is as much a civic necessity as it is an economic one (nsf.gov). In this way, proportionality respects difference in depth, while equity ensures no one is left out of the climb.

To declare that all must learn AI is not enough; institutions and systems must be held accountable for making it possible. Accountability with teeth requires measurable goals for AI literacy, resources committed to underserved communities, and transparent reporting on progress. Continuous improvement ensures that AI curricula evolve alongside the technology itself-today's literacy may focus on generative AI and data ethics, while tomorrow's may involve quantum-AI convergence or autonomous systems. The U.S. General Services Administration's performance-driven governance model offers a guide: adapt oversight and training frameworks in real time to meet emerging needs (coe.gsa.gov). In practice, this means AI literacy programs must be iterative, flexible, and deeply responsive to feedback from learners and communities. To answer who must learn AI is, ultimately, to affirm that every stakeholder-students, faculty, employers, policymakers, and citizens-deserves a seat in the classroom of the future.

The imperative to engage with AI in both critical and exploratory spaces begins with purpose. If education and workforce institutions retreat from this engagement, others-commercial actors, unregulated platforms, or opportunistic interests-will define the terrain. To honor our mission of expanding opportunity and safeguarding dignity, we must ensure that learners, faculty, and communities have the tools to critically evaluate AI and the courage to explore its potential. The U.S. Department of Education's AI policy guidance underscores this need by emphasizing that responsible engagement is essential to equity, access, and innovation (tech.ed.gov). Critical engagement allows us to interrogate AI's biases, limitations, and ethical risks; exploratory engagement allows us to discover new pedagogies, research pathways, and workforce applications. To do one without the other is insufficient-mission alignment demands that both critique and exploration converge in service of people, not just systems.

Engaging critically and exploratorily also requires proportionality and equity. Different communities bear different risks and opportunities, and governance must balance these realities. For underserved populations, critical engagement ensures AI systems are scrutinized for bias, exclusion, or inequitable outcomes; exploratory engagement ensures these same populations can access AI's promise in new workforce pathways, improved healthcare, or accessible learning tools.

Equity-by-design means structuring research, curricula, and innovation hubs so that historically marginalized voices are not simply "included" but centered in the design process. Defense-in-depth guarantees that safeguards-policy, technical checks, and human oversight-are in place as we experiment and explore. Georgia's AI governance principles make this clear: responsible AI requires ongoing assessment of both harms and opportunities (ai.georgia.gov). To engage in convergence is to recognize risk and possibility as partners, not adversaries, in the climb.

Engagement without accountability risks becoming performative. Institutions must not only host conversations about AI's critical and exploratory frontiers-they must act on what is learned. Accountability with teeth requires naming leaders responsible for shepherding critical analysis into policy and exploratory findings into practice.

Continuous improvement ensures that this process is not episodic but ongoing, with findings from classrooms, labs, and communities feeding back into governance and policy cycles. The U.S. General Services Administration stresses adaptive governance that evolves alongside technology, urging leaders to treat engagement as iterative rather than conclusive (coe.gsa.gov). Communities who never chose to climb will be shaped by how we choose to engage now. Our responsibility is to show that engagement-both critical and exploratory-is not an indulgence but a duty: a disciplined posture of questioning and curiosity that protects justice while cultivating opportunity.

The obligation to define training and learning that is adoptable, portable, scalable, useful, and universal begins with a mission-centered perspective. Our task is not simply to create programs that serve niche learners or privileged geographies, but to design systems of knowledge that reach across communities, industries, and contexts. Mission-first alignment demands that learning models are tied directly to student success, workforce transformation, and community resilience. The U.S. Department of Education emphasizes that innovation in learning must be aligned with equity and the expansion of access to opportunity (tech.ed.gov). If training does not strengthen pathways to upward mobility and workforce relevance, then it risks becoming another siloed experiment. Additionally, affected communities risk becoming deserted. Universal learning, therefore, is not about uniformity-it is about ensuring every learner, regardless of circumstance, has access to the skills and insights necessary to thrive in an AI-mediated future.

For training to be portable, scalable, and equitable, it must embrace proportionality: tailoring depth to need while guaranteeing baseline fluency for all. Basic AI literacy-understanding what AI is, where it is applied, and how to question it-should be universal, while specialized technical and governance competencies must be cultivated for educators, policymakers, and workforce leaders. Equity-by-design requires that rural communities, historically marginalized groups, and non-traditional learners are not only included, but prioritized in these efforts. Defense-in-depth ensures that as these learning ecosystems scale, protections remain in place: curricula must be tested for bias, training content must be transparent, and delivery mechanisms must be accessible across multiple modalities-online, hybrid, and in-person. The

National Science Foundation has argued that democratizing AI education is key to preparing society for both risk and opportunity (nsf.gov). Thus, universal training is not a race to standardize; it is a commitment to distribute knowledge and agency proportionally and justly.

Finally, the universality of AI training cannot be left to aspiration alone-it must be made enforceable through accountability and sustained through continuous improvement. Institutions must set measurable goals for adoption (number of learners reached), scalability (breadth of access across contexts), and usefulness (impact on employment, equity, and innovation outcomes). Accountability with teeth ensures leaders cannot claim success without transparent evidence of progress. Continuous improvement recognizes that AI and related technologies evolve quickly, meaning today's universal training frameworks must be updated and iterated tomorrow. The U.S. General Services Administration calls this "performance-driven governance," where evaluation and iteration are built into the structure itself (coe.gsa.gov). Training that is truly universal is therefore never static-it adapts alongside society, ensuring every learner is prepared not just for the now of work, but for the work yet to come. Students and future employees do not approach AI as an abstract concept-they encounter it as part of their daily lives, and they carry expectations shaped by that lived reality. Mission-first alignment obliges us to recognize these expectations not as consumer preferences but as signals of what responsible institutions must deliver.

Learners expect AI systems to enhance, not replace, human connection in the educational process. They want tools that make pathways clearer, reduce barriers, and accelerate achievement without diminishing the value of mentorship, creativity, or critical thinking. The U.S. Department of Education emphasizes that AI in learning environments should amplify opportunity and human flourishing rather than automate away care or judgment (tech.ed.gov). Likewise, employees entering the workforce expect AI to augment their performance, open new avenues of innovation, and build confidence that they are prepared for tomorrow's roles. To meet these expectations is to affirm that AI is in service to people, not people in service to AI.

Meeting expectations also requires proportionality and equity. Not all students will use AI the same way, and not all employees will encounter it under the same conditions. For some, expectations revolve around basic transparency-clear explanations of how AI influences grading, advising, or hiring. For others, especially in technical and creative fields, expectations include access to advanced AI tools that allow them to push the boundaries of their disciplines. Equity-by-design requires that these benefits are distributed fairly, ensuring that rural, first-generation, and historically underserved students are not left with diluted or outdated versions of AI-infused tools. Defense-in-depth guarantees that while systems are designed to delight and empower, they are also safeguarded against misuse, drift, or harm. Georgia's statewide AI principles underscore that public institutions must design for fairness and trustworthiness to sustain legitimacy (ai.georgia.gov). By embedding safeguards within delivery, institutions not only meet but exceed the expectations of students and employees.

Expectations evolve as fast as technology itself, and governance must keep pace. Accountability with teeth requires institutions to measure whether AI-infused systems are actually meeting the expectations they promise: Are students experiencing greater clarity in advising? Are employees finding AI tools that genuinely expand opportunities rather than automate them away? Continuous improvement ensures these questions are not rhetorical but operational-driving regular feedback cycles, system audits, and user-centered redesigns. The U.S. General Services Administration emphasizes that responsive governance adapts to changing stakeholder needs, rather than assuming yesterday's solutions will suffice today (coe.gsa.gov). Students and employees expect institutions to be not just adopters of AI but accountable stewards of its impact. Our responsibility is to meet those expectations with structures that are transparent, adaptive, and unrelentingly focused on human dignity and enduring success.

Employers increasingly view higher education not only as a place of discovery but also as a pipeline for workforce readiness. In an AI-enabled economy, their expectations are sharpened: they need graduates who understand how to work with, critique, and responsibly deploy AI in ways that advance productivity and innovation. Mission-first alignment requires higher education to frame this obligation not as transactional but as deeply connected to its broader purpose-equipping learners for great careers while cultivating adaptable, ethical citizens. The U.S. Department of Labor projects that AI-related job categories will expand across industries, from advanced manufacturing to healthcare, highlighting the need for responsive educational models (bls.gov). Employers demand that higher education serve as a partner, ensuring curricula, credentials, and research remain aligned with evolving industry realities. The mission, therefore, is dual: preparing students for work and ensuring that work contributes meaningfully to communities.

Employer needs also highlight the principle of proportionality. Not every program requires the same depth of AI integration, but every program must ensure its graduates possess baseline literacy. Engineering and data science students may require deep technical fluency, while business, healthcare, and social sciences students need critical understanding of AI's applications and limitations in their fields. Equity-by-design ensures that these opportunities are distributed fairly, not concentrated in elite institutions or urban centers. Employers consistently demand that graduates be diverse, inclusive, and representative of the populations they serve-meaning AI training must extend to rural and underserved learners as well. Defense-in-depth applies here, too: institutions must guarantee that as AI is integrated into teaching and learning, students are also trained in ethical use, bias mitigation, and system oversight. The National Science Foundation has emphasized that preparing the workforce requires attention to both technical skills and responsible use (nsf.gov). Meeting employer expectations, therefore, is not just about filling jobs but about cultivating trustworthy leaders who can navigate AI responsibly.

Employers will not accept promises without proof; they demand accountability. This means higher education must demonstrate outcomes through measurable competencies, validated credentials, and transparent pathways from classroom to workplace. Accountability with teeth requires that institutions track whether graduates are succeeding in AI-mediated environments, and whether training programs are reducing-not widening-equity gaps in workforce participation. Continuous improvement ensures alignment is not static but dynamic, with curricula and partnerships refreshed regularly to match the rapid evolution of industry needs. The U.S. General Services Administration underscores the importance of adaptive systems that evolve with technology, rather than being locked into outdated frameworks (coe.gsa.gov). Employers expect higher education to be both agile and reliable, delivering graduates who are future-ready and grounded in ethical stewardship. Our charge is to ensure that demand is not only met but exceeded, affirming higher education's role as both workforce partner and societal steward.

The mission of higher education and workforce development is not only to transmit knowledge but to cultivate human potential-creativity, trust, and dignity are central to that mission. As AI becomes embedded in classrooms, workplaces, and communities, we must ensure that it is not permitted to diminish these qualities but instead is leveraged to strengthen them. Mission-first alignment demands that institutions explicitly evaluate AI deployments against these values. Does an AI tool amplify the creativity of students and faculty, or does it reduce them to consumers of automated content? Does it build trust between learners, teachers, and employers, or does it introduce opacity and suspicion? Does it respect the dignity of individuals, particularly the vulnerable, or does it erode agency? The U.S. Department of Education's AI and the Future of Teaching and Learning policy guidance calls for AI to be human-centered, advancing the flourishing of learners rather than replacing human presence and care (tech.ed.gov). By grounding every adoption in this mission lens, institutions ensure that creativity, trust, and dignity are not casualties of progress but guiding stars.

Creativity thrives when learners are empowered with tools that extend imagination, not confine it. Proportionality requires that AI is scaled in ways that encourage innovation across disciplines-from arts and humanities to STEM-without privileging only the technical fields. Equity-by-design ensures that access to creative AI tools does not become the privilege of well-funded programs or elite institutions but is made available to rural schools, community colleges, and under-resourced learners. Trust, in this context, is cultivated by transparency: students and employees must know when AI is used, how it works, and where its limits lie. Defense-in-depth ensures that even as AI assists in creative processes or decision-making, humans remain in command to preserve dignity and accountability. Georgia's AI governance framework emphasizes fairness and explainability as prerequisites for trustworthy adoption (ai.georgia.gov). By layering safeguards into creative and operational ecosystems, institutions build confidence that AI is a collaborator rather than a competitor, a partner rather than a threat.

Finally, ensuring AI enhances rather than erodes creativity, trust, and dignity requires governance structures that are enforceable and adaptive. Accountability with teeth means institutions must measure whether AI tools demonstrably expand opportunities for creative expression, build trust in educational and workplace processes, and respect human dignity in deployment. This is not a matter of aspiration but of evidence-tracking outcomes, publishing transparent evaluations, and holding vendors, leaders, and faculty accountable when tools fall short. Continuous improvement ensures that governance evolves with AI itself; as new creative possibilities emerge, institutions must remain responsive, iterating on policies and practices to protect and promote human values. The U.S. General Services Administration underscores the necessity of adaptive governance that evolves alongside technology to maintain public confidence (coe.gsa.gov). The ultimate measure of success is not whether AI adoption is widespread, but whether it leaves communities more creative, more trusting, and more dignified than before. AI stewardship, then, is not only a technical obligation but a moral covenant.

Responsible failure in AI begins with a simple acknowledgment: all complex systems fail at some point. The question is not if but how, and whether those failures align with institutional missions of equity, learning, and trust. A responsible failure is one that is bounded by foresight, mitigated by design, and transparent to those affected. Mission-first alignment requires us to ensure that even when AI stumbles, students are not abandoned, employees are not unfairly penalized, and communities are not destabilized. As the U.S. Department of Education reminds us, the purpose of AI integration in learning is to expand opportunity and access (tech.ed.gov). Thus, failure must never come at the expense of access to care, guidance, or opportunity. If a tutoring bot misdirects, it must route quickly to a human; if a scheduling system falters, there must be a visible path to correction.

Mission-first alignment also requires that failure is framed as part of learning, not as a source of shame or abandonment. Students learn resilience when institutions model it: admitting failure, explaining it clearly, and showing how it will be fixed. This does not absolve organizations of responsibility-it deepens it. Failure becomes responsible when it is contextualized in mission terms: did the stumble cause harm, or did it reinforce the mission of dignity and opportunity by protecting against worse outcomes? When AI adoption is tied to institutional values, the very definition of failure shifts: failure is not when the technology falters but when human dignity is compromised. Responsible institutions will teach communities that failure is not a signal of incompetence but a marker of honest experimentation governed by principled safeguards.

Finally, mission-first alignment underscores that the communities most affected by failure are often those least equipped to recover quickly. If our mission is access and equity, then responsible failure must ensure recovery resources are built into governance. This could include financial aid extensions for students delayed by system errors, emergency retraining pathways for displaced workers, or communication protocols that explain what happened in clear, accessible language. When failures align with mission, recovery is not reactive but embedded as part of stewardship. In this sense, responsible failure becomes an extension of institutional care, demonstrating that even when systems stumble, the institution's commitment to its mission holds steady.

Who defines responsible failure is as important as how it is defined. If failure thresholds are set only by developers or vendors, they will often emphasize efficiency over equity, uptime over dignity. Proportionality ensures that definitions of failure are scaled to the consequence of the system in question:

a chatbot error may be an inconvenience, but bias in admissions or credentialing constitutes systemic harm. Institutions must set these thresholds in dialogue with communities, employers, and policymakers to ensure that definitions reflect lived realities, not just technical metrics. The GAO's AI accountability framework emphasizes that oversight must include stakeholder input, particularly where vulnerable populations are impacted (gao.gov). Responsible failure is therefore failure defined not unilaterally, but collaboratively.

Equity-by-design further requires that those who historically bear disproportionate harm from system failures-first-generation students, rural learners, underrepresented workers-are part of the governance process. If definitions of failure are not inclusive, institutions risk normalizing harm to those without voice. This is why proportionality must pair with equity: not every system needs the same scrutiny, but those that affect vulnerable groups require the strictest safeguards. Defense-in-depth then becomes the mechanism by which failure is rendered survivable. Multiple layers-technical audits, human review, policy guardrails-ensure that when one layer collapses, others catch the fallout. A failed grading algorithm should not result in a student's expulsion; oversight and appeal systems should intercept such errors before harm becomes irreversible.

Defense-in-depth also makes failure less about catastrophe and more about graceful recovery. When AI systems are monitored across layers, institutions can contain harm, learn from the error, and adjust without systemic collapse. For example, bias detected in a workforce-matching algorithm should trigger both technical recalibration and policy review, ensuring that communities regain trust not just in the system but in the institution's stewardship. Georgia's AI principles stress that fairness and accountability are inseparable: governance must both prevent and respond to inequities (ai.georgia.gov). By embedding safeguards that anticipate breakdown, institutions model a new kind of resilience-one where responsible failure is an expected, managed, and instructive part of system evolution.

Trust in organizations that define responsible failure cannot be assumed; it must be earned through accountability. Institutions that ask for trust without offering transparency will lose credibility. Accountability with teeth requires naming specific owners for AI systems, publishing metrics of both performance and failure, and instituting consequences when safeguards are ignored or harms exceed acceptable thresholds. Communities must be able to see that responsibility is not diffuse but concrete-that someone is answerable when AI fails. The Department of Homeland Security stresses the importance of human-centered, auditable AI systems as a foundation for trust in government use (dhs.gov). Higher education and workforce institutions must mirror this posture, creating mechanisms that give communities confidence in oversight.

Continuous improvement then transforms failure into a resource rather than a liability. Each failure becomes a feedback loop that refines safeguards, informs future design, and strengthens governance culture. Institutions that conceal or downplay failure deprive themselves of critical learning opportunities. Conversely, those that treat failure as part of an iterative cycle not only adapt more effectively but also model resilience to their communities. The U.S. General Services Administration's call for performance-driven governance reinforces this: policies and systems must evolve alongside technology to maintain legitimacy (coe.gsa.gov). Failure becomes irresponsible only when it is repeated without learning, or when it is hidden without accountability.

Finally, communities must be equipped to recover when failures occur. This requires more than technical fixes-it demands investment in recovery infrastructures: counseling for students, retraining funds for workers, communication channels that restore trust. Resilient communities are not accidental; they are built through intentional policy and investment. By embedding recovery resources into governance, institutions demonstrate that accountability is not punitive alone but restorative. Responsible failure, then, is not defined only by what goes wrong but by how quickly and fairly institutions make it right. Communities that see institutions fail transparently, recover responsibly, and improve iteratively are far more likely to extend trust and engage in shared stewardship.

For Tennessee's community colleges, ensuring meaningful voice begins with reaffirming the mission to advance access, equity, and workforce opportunity. Students across the TBR system-enrolling nearly 100,000 learners annually-often represent first-generation, low-income, rural, and adult re-entry populations. These groups are most directly shaped by AI adoption in advising, admissions, financial aid, and course delivery, yet historically they are least likely to be at the table when technologies are chosen or deployed. Mission-first alignment means that voice cannot be an afterthought-it must be a first principle. The Tennessee Higher Education Commission's (THEC) 2024 Fact Book shows that about 36% of community college students are first-generation learners and nearly 70% receive financial aid. These realities demand that systems designed to "assist" never unintentionally exclude or penalize the very populations they aim to serve. The U.S. Department of

Education echoes this point: technology must advance equity and opportunity (tech.ed.gov). For Tennessee, this means embedding student, faculty, and employer voices directly into the governance mission.

At Motlow State Community College, where more than 60% of students come from economically distressed or at-risk counties, mission alignment requires elevating rural and nontraditional learners as central stakeholders. Their experiences are distinct from those of students in larger urban institutions: broadband access may be limited, workforce pathways are tied to regional employers, and community support structures differ. To ensure meaningful voice, institutions like Motlow must continue to create advisory boards, listening sessions, and pilot programs where these students and communities shape AI adoption before deployment. Mission alignment reframes voice as stewardship: technology must reflect not only what institutions think students need but also what students, employers, and communities say they need.

Finally, mission-first alignment calls for linking voice directly to Tennessee's Drive to 55 initiative, which aims to ensure 55% of Tennesseans earn a postsecondary credential. If AI adoption excludes or alienates vulnerable learners, the state's central mission is undermined. By contrast, when voices of those most affected are included, AI can accelerate credential completion, increase workforce placement, and support long-term economic development. In this way, mission alignment ensures that meaningful voice is not symbolic but measurable-tied to outcomes that advance statewide goals of opportunity and prosperity.

Not all AI systems carry equal risk, and proportionality requires that the systems most likely to impact student access, aid, or workforce opportunity must carry the highest expectations for meaningful voice. For instance, an AI advising chatbot at Motlow that helps students register for classes should include input from students who often struggle with enrollment "melt." THEC data shows that nearly 20% of Tennessee community college applicants fail to complete enrollment due to barriers in the admissions pipeline. Without student voice, AI systems may inadvertently reinforce those barriers instead of breaking them down. By contrast, a classroom scheduling tool may warrant lighter consultation. Proportionality ensures that voice is scaled to consequence, preserving agility while embedding equity where risk is greatest.

Equity-by-design insists that participation is representative of Tennessee's student population. Across TBR institutions, 48% of community college students are

Pell-eligible, and over 40% identify as nontraditional learners (over age 25). These groups disproportionately bear the risks of exclusion when AI systems automate advising, credentialing, or financial aid. Ensuring equity means actively recruiting these voices into governance councils and community advisory groups. For example, Motlow's recent AI literacy survey-completed by over 1,000 students, faculty, and staff in 2025-revealed that first-generation students expressed more skepticism about AI than peers, largely due to concerns about fairness in grading and access to advisors. These findings emphasize that equity requires institutions to center skepticism, not silence it, ensuring governance addresses fears as well as aspirations.

Defense-in-depth then secures voice through redundancy. Students might participate in Motlow's Student Government Association, contribute to statewide advisory councils convened by TBR, and have access to grievance mechanisms that feed directly into AI oversight boards. If one channel is ignored, another provides an avenue for expression. Georgia's AI guidelines stress the importance of layered accountability (ai.georgia.gov), and Tennessee can operationalize this by ensuring every AI adoption is subject to both local (college-level) and system-wide (TBR/THEC) consultation. This defense-in-depth model guarantees that voice is not tokenized-it is institutionalized across multiple levels of governance.

Commitment without currency is counterfeit as a colleague once shared, and so is Voice. Voice without accountability is empty. Institutions must demonstrate not only that input was collected but also that it shaped decisions. At TBR and THEC, this can mean publishing transparent reports showing how student, faculty, and community feedback influenced AI adoption policies and practices. For instance, if rural students at Motlow identify broadband limitations as a barrier, accountability requires documenting how that input changes AI implementation plans (e.g., ensuring offline or hybrid models are available). Accountability with teeth also demands measurable goals: percentage of AI governance decisions informed by community feedback, representation of Pell-eligible or first-generation students in advisory roles, and response times for addressing grievances. The Department of Homeland Security emphasizes that human-centered, auditable systems are foundational to trust (dhs.gov). Tennessee institutions must carry this forward by making accountability enforceable, not optional.

Continuous improvement ensures that governance evolves as AI and communities change. THEC's labor statistics demonstrate that Tennessee's workforce is rapidly shifting toward advanced manufacturing, healthcare, and IT-industries where AI adoption is most pronounced. As these shifts occur, governance must regularly revisit which voices are most affected and ensure their inclusion. Motlow's AI Summit (launched in 2025) serves as a model of adaptive governance: bringing students, faculty, employers, and community partners together to review progress and recalibrate strategies annually. The U.S. General Services Administration stresses this adaptive, performance-driven governance as essential to sustaining legitimacy (coe.gsa.gov). Tennessee's approach must mirror this-ensuring that voice is not a static checkbox but a living system of engagement.

Finally, accountability must extend into recovery. When AI systems fail-whether in admissions, advising, or workforce placement-affected communities must not only be informed but also included in shaping remediation. This could mean creating recovery grants for students delayed by AI errors, retraining programs for displaced workers, or public forums to process and repair trust. Motlow's resilience in responding to student needs during past crises (from natural disasters to economic downturns) demonstrates that recovery can strengthen rather than weaken community bonds when handled transparently. Embedding recovery into governance ensures that meaningful voice is present not just in adoption but in restoration, reinforcing trust in institutions as true stewards of technology and community.

Preserving human judgment begins with the mission: higher education and workforce systems exist not only to transmit knowledge but to cultivate discernment, ethical reasoning, and wisdom. In Tennessee, where TBR institutions serve nearly 100,000 learners annually, the responsibility is clear: AI must support-not supplant-human capacity to judge, decide, and create. The Tennessee Higher Education Commission's 2024 Fact Book shows that over 70% of community college students are employed while enrolled, balancing school, work, and family responsibilities (tn.gov/thec). Their lived experiences are full of embodied decision-making-navigating time, resources, and obligations-that no algorithm can replicate. Mission-first alignment means ensuring AI systems offer support without undermining the very human skill of judgment.

Creativity, too, is central to the mission. Students at Motlow and across Tennessee's community colleges learn not only technical skills but also the creative problem-solving that employers demand. AI can enhance this by automating repetitive tasks, freeing space for higher-order thinking, but it can also constrain creativity if misused as a shortcut for thought. The U.S. Department of Education emphasizes that AI adoption in classrooms must strengthen-not weaken-critical thinking and creative exploration (tech.ed.gov). Mission alignment requires designing AI-infused learning that prompts students to ask deeper questions, experiment boldly, and generate original solutions. Creativity preserved in this way is not ornamental-it is the heart of workforce readiness.

Embodied wisdom-rooted in lived experience, cultural traditions, and human interaction-cannot be encoded fully into algorithms. In rural Tennessee communities, wisdom often flows through intergenerational knowledge, workplace mentorship, and community storytelling. Mission-first alignment insists that AI must amplify this embodied wisdom, not replace it. For example, in healthcare programs, simulation technology can train decision-making, but only human judgment guided by empathy and ethical care ensures dignity in practice. Preserving embodied wisdom means building systems that listen to human context, not overwrite it. In this way, mission-first governance affirms that judgment, creativity, and wisdom are not inefficiencies to be optimized away but the very essence of learning and leadership.

Proportionality requires institutions to calibrate AI's role carefully: use it to extend human judgment and creativity, but not to dominate decision-making. For example, AI tools in admissions or advising may assist with identifying trends or generating options, but final decisions must rest with human advisors who understand individual student contexts. Tennessee Board of Regents data shows that over 60% of students at community colleges enroll part-time, often due to work or family demands (tbr.edu). A purely data-driven system might view these learners as "at risk," but human advisors can recognize resilience, ambition, and potential beyond the metrics. Proportionality ensures that human judgment remains the ultimate authority in decisions with profound personal impact.

Equity-by-design emphasizes that creativity and embodied wisdom must be preserved not only for the privileged but for all learners. Students in rural and distressed counties often lack access to cutting-edge technology, yet their creative resilience-balancing multiple jobs, supporting family enterprises, and contributing to community well-being-reflects a wisdom that AI cannot replicate. AI systems must be designed to respect and amplify this diversity of experience. Motlow's AI Literacy Survey in 2025 revealed that students value AI tools most when they enhance-not replace-human mentorship and creativity. Equity requires that AI systems foster, rather than flatten, the distinctive ways communities learn and innovate.

Defense-in-depth protects human-centered values through layered safeguards. For example, in workforce credentialing, AI might propose skill matches for manufacturing or healthcare jobs, but defense-in-depth ensures that human oversight reviews cultural fit, growth potential, and dignity in placement. Georgia's AI governance guidelines emphasize fairness and explainability, reminding us that no algorithm should operate without transparent reasoning (ai.georgia.gov). By embedding human checkpoints at every stage, defense-in-depth preserves judgment, creativity, and wisdom. AI becomes a collaborator, not a substitute, ensuring human faculties remain at the center of innovation.

Accountability with teeth requires institutions to demonstrate that AI adoption is actively preserving-not eroding-human creativity, judgment, and dignity. This means measuring outcomes beyond efficiency: Are students demonstrating stronger critical thinking skills? Do employers report that graduates retain the creativity and adaptability demanded by the workplace? THEC workforce data shows that Tennessee's fastest-growing fields-advanced manufacturing, healthcare, and IT-list creativity, teamwork, and problem-solving as top employability skills. Accountability ensures institutions do not drift toward producing efficient but unimaginative workers. Metrics must reflect human capacities, not just system performance.

Continuous improvement acknowledges that preserving human creativity and wisdom is not a one-time design choice but an ongoing process. Institutions must create feedback loops where students, faculty, and employers assess whether AI tools are enabling or constraining human potential. Motlow's AI Summit (2025) modeled this approach, inviting broad stakeholder input to refine adoption strategies. The U.S. General Services Administration stresses adaptive governance-policies must evolve alongside systems to remain effective (coe.gsa.gov). By embedding iteration into governance, Tennessee institutions can ensure that AI tools are recalibrated when they drift from supporting human-centered outcomes.

Finally, accountability and improvement must extend to communities themselves. Preserving embodied wisdom means not only listening to student and faculty voices but also engaging parents, employers, and local leaders. Rural employers in Middle Tennessee, for instance, emphasize the value of work ethic, creativity, and human connection in addition to technical skill. By institutionalizing their voices in governance councils and policy reviews, institutions affirm that AI must enhance-not erase-these qualities. Systems that are accountable to communities are more likely to build trust, resilience, and legitimacy. In this way, governance becomes more than compliance: it becomes stewardship of humanity itself in an AI-mediated world.

As we step into this next phase, let us carry forward the conviction that AI must remain a servant to human flourishing- not the other way around. We are no longer only innovators; we are custodians. Our charge is not just to advance what AI can do, but to ensure that what it does leaves the world more just, more connected, and more capable than it found it. Am I naive? Am I spending too much time alone thinking through these concepts? Perhaps, but …

We planted the trees. Now we must tend the forest.

References - Chapter 2

1. Tennessee Board of Regents. Fast Facts and System Reports, 2024-2025. tbr.edu

2. Tennessee Higher Education Commission. 2024-2025 Tennessee Higher Education Fact Book. tn.gov/thec

3. Motlow State Community College. AI Literacy Survey Results, Fall 2025. (Internal Report)

4. U.S. Department of Education, Office of Educational Technology. Artificial Intelligence and the Future of Teaching and Learning: Policy Guidance. tech.ed.gov

5. State of Georgia. Guidelines for State Organizations on AI. ai.georgia.gov

6. U.S. General Services Administration, Centers of Excellence. AI Guide for Government: Responsible Implementation. coe.gsa.gov

7. National Science Foundation. Future of Artificial Intelligence Research and Education. nsf.gov

8. U.S. Bureau of Labor Statistics. Occupational Outlook Handbook: Computer and Information Research Scientists, and Related AI Occupations. bls.gov

9. U.S. Department of Education, Office of Educational Technology. Advancing Equity and Opportunity with EdTech. tech.ed.gov

10. U.S. Government Accountability Office. Artificial Intelligence: An Accountability Framework. gao.gov

11. U.S. Department of Homeland Security. Ensuring AI is Used Responsibly. dhs.gov

Chapter 3 - Human in the loop ...

When the pace of technological change accelerates, there is a quiet but dangerous temptation to let the machines decide. This is wrong, IMHO. The logic is beguiling: do we not hear that common refrain of "algorithms are faster, data-driven, unburdened by fatigue or bias." But the truth is more complicated. Machines are not free from bias; they are mirrors of the humans who train them. They are reflections of sociocultural empathy-or lack thereof-as a continuum of pasts, presents, and future possibilities. As we (humans) are not impermeable to "feel" and "emote," nor are we immutable to contexts and our own lineages, perspectives, teaching, and maxims, so too are machines subject to error. They inherit the limits of the datasets we feed them. Even fatigue and burnout have their corollaries in system degradation, model drift, and bias accumulation. Moreover, machines are not accountable-unless we make them so. And should we? That is why the concept of the human in the loop must be more than a technical safeguard in AI systems. It must be a philosophical anchor.

Are we not moving from safeguards to ethos? In engineering, a "human in the loop" is a control point-the person who must approve, override, or adjust a machine's output before it moves forward. In a broader societal sense, it is a recognition that human values, judgment, and empathy are irreplaceable in governance, learning, and problem-solving. We can program malfunction responses, but programmable logic does not think; it compares inputs to outputs without moral reasoning.

In Tennessee, where the Tennessee Board of Regents (TBR) system educates nearly 100,000 community college students annually, many of them first-generation and Pell-eligible (tbr.edu), the ethos of humanism is not abstract-it is lived. These students need advisors who can discern unspoken anxieties, instructors who can adjust lessons to context, and communities that see them as more than data points. The Tennessee Higher Education Commission (THEC) reports that over 70% of community college students balance work while studying, requiring advisors to interpret far more than GPA (tn.gov/thec). AI can assist, but only humans can empathize, encourage, and guide in ways that align with mission.

In education, the human in the loop is the teacher who adapts an AI-generated lesson to match a student's emotional state that day. In workforce training, it is the mentor who can read the unspoken anxieties of a learner shifting into a new career field. Our work with Metaversity and micro-credentialing proves that the most effective digital systems are those that augment human connection rather than replace it. The blockchain can verify a skill; only a human can encourage its application in a way that honors the learner's aspirations.

THEC's labor reports project Tennessee's fastest-growing jobs in healthcare, advanced manufacturing, and IT (tn.gov/thec). These fields demand not only technical competence but also creativity, adaptability, and teamwork. Motlow's AI Literacy Survey (2025) confirmed that students most value AI tools when they supplement mentorship, not substitute for it. Our students, when informally engaged, discuss the clarity, deconstructive, and search capability as useful advantages of AI. AI can organize, but humans contextualize; AI can recommend, but humans inspire. If we strip the loop of its human anchors, we risk a workforce that is technically skilled but humanly diminished. Global AI networks introduce new complexity: the loop is now distributed across borders. A content moderation decision in Nairobi may affect a student in Nashville; a hiring algorithm in Munich may source candidates from Manila. Accountability in this distributed loop demands:

1. Multi-jurisdictional oversight that respects sovereignty while enabling interoperability.

2. Transparency protocols so individuals can understand and challenge algorithmic decisions.

3. Cultural adaptation layers in AI systems to ensure relevance and respect to local norms.

NIST's AI Risk Management Framework emphasizes layered accountability to preserve human judgment even in distributed systems (nist.gov). Similarly, UNESCO's Recommendation on the Ethics of AI stresses global human rights as a design imperative (unesco.org). In Tennessee, this translates into trust networks that give students agency over their credentials and communities visibility into how systems shape opportunity. Where do we begin to explore trust networks and credentials?

In trust networks-credentialing platforms, public data exchanges, cross-sector coalitions-the quality of relationships matters as much as the integrity of the algorithms. Our Tennessee experience shows that trust grows when stakeholders have visibility into how systems are built, when communities have voice in shaping those systems, and when learners have choice in how their data and credentials are shared. Each principle is a building block for ensuring AI serves as a tool of empowerment rather than erosion.

Visibility is the first principle of trust. Without clear understanding of how AI systems function, stakeholders are left to suspicion, doubt, or disengagement. According to McKinsey's State of AI 2024 report, only 23% of organizations say they have "full visibility" into their AI models and decision-making processes, yet those that do report significantly higher trust and adoption rates (mckinsey.com). In higher education and workforce contexts, visibility requires clear documentation of how AI tools are trained, what data sources are used, and how decisions are validated.

In Tennessee, visibility is an operational necessity. When Motlow piloted blockchain-based micro-credentials, employer partners were not merely end-users but active observers of the verification process. They could see how skills were defined, verified, and mapped to workforce competencies. This transparency increased employer confidence and ensured students knew their achievements would be recognized. Similarly, Brookings emphasizes that human-in-the-loop transparency builds resilience and public legitimacy in education systems adopting AI (brookings.edu). Visibility moves trust from abstract principle to operational reality: not "trust us," but "see with us."

WHO underscores this point in the healthcare domain, arguing that transparency in AI systems is non-negotiable when human well-being is at stake (who.int). Education and workforce AI systems must carry the same ethic. Stakeholders-from faculty to policymakers-need dashboards, reports, and governance channels that make AI visible and interpretable. Only then can relationships of trust sustain innovation across Tennessee and beyond.

Voice is co-authorship. Communities most affected by AI systems cannot be passive recipients; they must actively shape them. Gartner's 2023 AI Governance Survey found that organizations with structured stakeholder engagement in AI governance were 40% more likely to report higher trust in outcomes (gartner.com). Voice ensures AI reflects the lived experiences and values of the people it serves, not just the assumptions of technical developers or corporate vendors.

In Tennessee, community voice has been a decisive factor in successful workforce innovation. THEC's engagement with rural communities demonstrates that training programs gain higher participation rates when local leaders and employers shape curriculum design. At Motlow, student advisory boards have informed how
AI-assisted advising is implemented-highlighting barriers like broadband

access and cultural fit that algorithms alone would miss. This aligns with Brookings' observation that participatory governance prevents AI from reinforcing inequities by surfacing perspectives often left out of traditional design processes (brookings.edu).

Global frameworks echo this imperative. WHO's Ethics and Governance of Artificial Intelligence for Health stresses that communities must have channels for deliberation and grievance when AI affects their lives, particularly vulnerable groups (who.int).
For Tennessee and the TBR system, this means institutionalizing advisory councils, public comment periods, and grievance redress mechanisms that make voice permanent. When communities see their concerns directly shape AI governance, trust is not symbolic-it becomes institutionalized.

Choice is the ultimate measure of agency in trust networks. Learners must not only know how their data is used but also control how it is shared. UNESCO's Recommendation on the Ethics of AI identifies data sovereignty and individual agency as essential for protecting dignity in AI ecosystems (unesco.org). Without choice, learners risk being subsumed into systems where credentials are commodified without their consent. With choice, they become empowered actors in shaping their educational and workforce futures.
Motlow's blockchain-based credentialing pilots illustrate this principle in action. Students can selectively share verified credentials with employers, transfer institutions, or licensing boards. This flexibility aligns with McKinsey's research showing that portable, interoperable credentials increase worker mobility and employer confidence (mckinsey.com). It also reduces "data silos" that often trap learners in institutional or vendor-controlled ecosystems. Choice transforms credentials from static transcripts into dynamic instruments of opportunity.

Equity depends on this agency. Gartner predicts that by 2027, over 60% of AI-driven credentialing systems will require explicit consent and learner-controlled sharing mechanisms (gartner.com). For vulnerable populations-such as veterans, foster youth, or justice-involved learners-control over disclosure can prevent stigma while still enabling opportunity. WHO warns that unchecked AI-driven data flows can reinforce inequities, particularly when applied to marginalized groups (who.int). By embedding choice, Tennessee's trust networks show how governance can protect dignity while expanding opportunity. Learners are not just part of the loop-they hold the keys to it.

This is why universally integrated systems (UIS) must evolve not toward fully automated credential economies but toward human-validated, culturally grounded skill ecosystems. As Brookings scholars note, creative human judgment is America's comparative edge in education and workforce in the age of AI (brookings.edu). Scaling this globally requires governance architectures that make humanism the default, not the exception.

The human in the loop is not a brake on progress; it is the steering wheel. Without it, we risk being passengers in systems that take us where we never intended to go. As we step further into universally integrated education-workforce networks, blockchain-verified trust systems, and AI-mediated civic life, the challenge will be ensuring that every loop-local, national, global-is anchored in human judgment, human ethics, and human care. The measure of our AI systems will not be their raw computational power, but their ability to extend dignity, opportunity, and creativity to more people, in more places, with fewer barriers. And that, more than any technical achievement, will define whether AI's legacy is one of empowerment or erosion.

Humans are the alpha and omega of the loops ...

References - Chapter 3

1. Tennessee Board of Regents. Fast Facts and System Reports, 2024-2025. tbr.edu

2. Tennessee Higher Education Commission. 2024-2025 Tennessee Higher Education Fact Book. tn.gov/thec

3. Motlow State Community College. AI Literacy Survey Results, Fall 2025. (Internal Report)

4. U.S. Department of Education, Office of Educational Technology. Artificial Intelligence and the Future of Teaching and Learning: Policy Guidance. tech.ed.gov

5. National Institute of Standards and Technology (NIST). AI Risk Management Framework. nist.gov

6. UNESCO. Recommendation on the Ethics of Artificial Intelligence. unesco.org

7. Brookings Institution. Creative Patterns in the Age of AI: Securing America's Education Edge. brookings.edu

8. Tennessee Board of Regents. Fast Facts and System Reports, 2024-2025. tbr.edu

9. Tennessee Higher Education Commission. 2024-2025 Tennessee Higher Education Fact Book. tn.gov/thec

10. Motlow State Community College. AI Literacy Survey Results, Fall 2025. (Internal Report)

11. World Health Organization. Ethics and Governance of Artificial Intelligence for Health. who.int

12. McKinsey & Company. The State of AI in 2024. mckinsey.com

13. Brookings Institution. Making AI Work for Schools. brookings.edu

14. Gartner. AI Governance Survey 2023. gartner.com

15. UNESCO. Recommendation on the Ethics of Artificial Intelligence. unesco.org

Chapter 4 - Now Meets Next: The Critical Decade for AI, Governance, and Global Trust

The first wave of AI integration was about proving possibilities. Could it work? Could it teach, translate, predict, simulate, and diagnose? That wave has passed. We are now in the second wave - not merely proving capability, but deciding how the capabilities will be governed, by whom, and for whose benefit. This decade is pivotal because the rules we set now - or fail to set - will calcify into norms, practices, and expectations that will be nearly impossible to undo by 2035. McKinsey estimates that AI could add $13 trillion to global GDP by 2030, but cautions that without coordinated governance, benefits will be unevenly distributed, widening inequities (mckinsey.com). The stakes are nothing less than global legitimacy and trust.

From National Agendas to Global Stakes

In Volume I, we wrestled with questions of privacy, blockchain verification, and policy/guidance in national and state contexts. Personally and professionally, I am still wrestling with the aforementioned. Newness brings fluidity and fluctuation, which is both exhilarating and numbing. Moreover, we worked within Tennessee's educational ecosystem, influenced regional workforce pathways, and contributed to U.S. discussions on credentialing and open education. Now, the conversations are moving into rooms where international interoperability and digital sovereignty dominate.

The European Union's AI Act (adopted in 2024) is setting global precedents for risk classification, transparency, and accountability (europa.eu). The African Union is developing continent-wide frameworks on AI ethics and cross-border data governance. The United Nations, through UNESCO and the Office of the Secretary-General's AI Advisory Body, is advancing recommendations for AI safety and human rights alignment. The WHO has called for global guardrails in health AI, warning that without international coordination, AI could reinforce inequities in healthcare access and outcomes (who.int). What we decide in the next ten years will determine whether AI becomes a global commons or a fragmented patchwork of incompatible, competing systems. We would not do that, would we?

Perhaps there is an interdependence dilemma. Global AI integration faces a paradox that cannot be resolved by technology alone. It is a tension between the necessity of shared standards and the equally pressing necessity of local adaptability. If we err too far toward uniformity, we risk flattening the human texture of culture and context. If we err too far toward fragmentation, we risk stalling innovation and reinforcing inequality. The paradox is not a flaw to be solved but a reality to be governed. We need shared standards for trust, safety, and interoperability.

Standards are the scaffolding of trust. Without common rules for safety, transparency, and accountability, AI systems cannot operate across borders or institutions. The European Union's AI Act provides the clearest example of this approach, offering a risk-based framework that classifies AI applications and mandates requirements for high-risk systems (europa.eu). This move is not just regulatory-it is diplomatic, establishing norms that others must respond to. McKinsey estimates that standardized governance could unlock trillions in cross-border AI value by 2030, while fragmented approaches could cost over $1 trillion annually in lost productivity (mckinsey.com).

The WHO echoes this need for shared standards in healthcare, warning that AI without globally recognized safety and equity protocols could deepen health disparities (who.int). If one nation demands transparency in diagnostic tools while another does not, the result is mistrust in cross-border care and stunted global health collaboration. Gartner reinforces this argument, predicting that by 2027, 60% of organizations will face interoperability failures in AI deployment if standards remain fragmented (gartner.com).

Brookings adds a cultural lens, noting that standards serve as the "lingua franca" of trust in an AI-mediated world (brookings.edu). Standards do not erase differences; they create the table where differences can be negotiated. To govern AI responsibly, we must accept that shared standards are not an optional layer of bureaucracy-they are the infrastructure of legitimacy in the global AI age. We also need local adaptability to honor cultural, economic, and political contexts. Yet if governance leans too heavily toward rigid standards, it risks suffocating the very diversity it must protect. AI cannot succeed as a one-size-fits-all project.

Cultural, economic, and political contexts shape how technology is understood, trusted, and adopted. UNESCO's Recommendation on the Ethics of AI stresses this balance, insisting that universal principles must be interpreted through local contexts to protect dignity and cultural identity (unesco.org).

Consider education and workforce development. In Tennessee, AI credentialing systems must account for rural broadband limitations, the needs of first-generation learners, and the realities of regional employers. These local dynamics differ from those in urban Berlin, rural Kenya, or industrial Guangzhou. Brookings notes that ignoring local nuance risks creating AI systems that are technically sound but socially illegitimate, eroding trust and adoption. WHO similarly underscores adaptability in healthcare: AI-driven diagnostic tools must be calibrated to local disease burdens, population health data, and health system capacity, or they risk producing inaccurate outcomes when exported uncritically across regions. McKinsey amplifies this point economically: countries that tailor AI adoption to their workforce realities are far more likely to achieve inclusive growth, while those that import models wholesale risk exacerbating unemployment and inequality.

Adaptability is not a threat to global standards-it is their proving ground. Standards provide the frame; adaptability fills it with human context. Gartner calls this the "dual-track" of governance: global coherence with local responsiveness. Without adaptability, AI systems may comply with regulation but fail in practice, rejected by the very communities they aim to serve. With adaptability, AI becomes not just a tool of efficiency but a bridge of equity, meeting global obligations while honoring local identities.

If global governance becomes too rigid, it risks erasing local nuance and enforcing a one-size-fits-none model. If it becomes too fragmented, we risk "AI silos" where innovation and data stay locked within national borders, slowing progress and reinforcing inequality. Gartner warns that by 2027, 60% of organizations will struggle with "AI interoperability gaps" caused by fragmented standards and regulations (gartner.com).

The challenge - and opportunity - is to design governance architectures that are both interoperable and adaptable. Brookings argues that this requires treating governance as diplomacy: balancing global standards with cultural pluralism (brookings.edu). This is not only a technical challenge; it is also a deeply human one, requiring political negotiation, cultural humility, and relational trust.

In this decade, trust will become the defining infrastructure of the AI era-every bit as essential as fiber optic cables, power grids, or highways. Unlike those physical infrastructures, trust is not poured in concrete or wired in copper. It is built through relationships, governance, and accountability. Without trust, the most advanced AI systems will stall in adoption, fracture across borders, and spark resistance rather than confidence. With trust, AI can accelerate innovation while safeguarding dignity, equity, and opportunity. If trusts breaks, nations will wall off their AI systems from one another.

When trust erodes, nations respond with protectionism. Instead of building interoperable systems, governments wall off their AI infrastructure to guard against perceived risks. The European Union's AI Act already sets global precedents for risk-based regulation, requiring high-risk applications (like biometric surveillance and healthcare AI) to meet strict obligations before deployment (europa.eu). While this increases trust within the EU, it also introduces barriers to non-EU partners unless mutual recognition agreements are forged. Without such agreements, AI ecosystems risk fragmentation. McKinsey notes that "AI nationalism" could slow global productivity gains by more than $1 trillion annually by limiting cross-border data flows and interoperability (mckinsey.com). Similarly, Brookings warns that fragmented AI regimes will entrench digital inequities, creating "data-rich" and "data-poor" zones across the globe (brookings.edu). WHO has raised parallel concerns in healthcare: if nations silo health AI systems, breakthroughs in diagnostics or pandemic response may be delayed or restricted, worsening inequities (who.int).

The lesson is clear: governance must prevent mistrust from hardening into borders. Global frameworks-like UNESCO's Recommendation on the Ethics of AI-seek to create shared principles, but operational mechanisms are needed to ensure interoperability. Without trust, we will not only fragment AI but also fracture the potential for global cooperation in addressing shared challenges like climate change, health, and security.

The thought of businesses hesitating to engage in cross-border AI commerce is plausible. Trust is also the currency of commerce. Businesses are more likely to adopt and scale AI systems when they trust that contracts, data-sharing agreements, and regulatory frameworks are stable and predictable. Gartner predicts that by 2027, 70% of cross-border AI commerce will hinge on verified trust protocols, such as transparent model documentation, interoperable standards, and enforceable data agreements (gartner.com). Without these safeguards, firms will retreat to domestic markets, stalling the growth of global AI economies.

McKinsey's State of AI 2024 report highlights this risk: while 60% of companies report experimenting with generative AI, fewer than 25% have scaled it globally, citing concerns over regulatory inconsistencies and data sovereignty (mckinsey.com). EU data supports this hesitation: European SMEs report that compliance with divergent AI standards across jurisdictions raises costs and slows innovation, even as demand for AI-enabled services grows (ec.europa.eu).

Brookings emphasizes that businesses are not only concerned about compliance but about reputation. Companies that deploy AI without trusted frameworks risk losing consumer confidence if harms occur-such as biased hiring tools, unsafe autonomous systems, or opaque financial algorithms. WHO's guidance in digital health echoes this, stressing that businesses will be more willing to scale AI solutions across borders if they can demonstrate compliance with trusted international norms (who.int). Trust, then, is not a brake on commerce; it is the infrastructure that makes commerce possible in the first place.

Citizens will resist adoption of AI-mediated services. At the most local level, trust determines whether citizens embrace or resist AI. Even the most sophisticated AI systems cannot succeed if citizens view them as illegitimate or unsafe. According to Gartner's Digital Trust Survey, nearly 48% of citizens globally say they "distrust" AI-mediated services unless clear accountability and transparency measures are in place (gartner.com). Without trust, resistance emerges in the form of protests, lawsuits, political pushback, or quiet non-use.

WHO's work on digital health underscores this risk: communities are unlikely to adopt AI-driven diagnostics if they believe the systems are biased, inaccessible, or designed without local input. This is particularly true in the Global South, where distrust of international systems is tied to histories of exploitation (who.int). Similarly, Brookings notes that trust gaps in AI adoption mirror historical inequities in education and technology access (brookings.edu). Without deliberate efforts to build citizen confidence, AI adoption risks reinforcing mistrust and widening divides.

The EU's Digital Compass 2030 strategy illustrates a different path: by embedding digital rights, transparent oversight, and citizen agency into AI and digital transformation plans, it seeks to cultivate citizen trust as the foundation of adoption (ec.europa.eu). McKinsey supports this argument, finding that citizens are far more likely to accept AI-mediated services when human oversight, explainability, and grievance mechanisms are present. Trust, at the citizen level, is built not only through safeguards but through daily experiences of fairness, care, and responsiveness. We know that building trust requires, but is not limited to the following ...

1. Verification Systems - Credential and identity systems that work across borders without sacrificing local control. The EU's European Digital

Identity Wallet pilot is one example of interoperability with sovereignty (europa.eu).

2. Transparency Protocols - Shared rules for explainability and auditability of AI decisions. WHO insists that healthcare AI must include transparent audit trails to build trust across health systems.

3. Data Sovereignty Agreements - Clear terms on where data can be stored, how it can be processed, and under whose legal jurisdiction. Brookings has warned that failure to reconcile sovereignty with interoperability risks splintering the digital economy into regional blocs.

Now is the time to dig into the governance triad. Trust, in this framing, is not a soft value. It is hard infrastructure, foundational to AI's scalability and legitimacy. Without trust embedded into governance, AI becomes brittle-technically advanced yet socially fragile. The governance triad-governments, industry coalitions, and civil society networks-deserves more than passing acknowledgment. These are not side players; they are the three legs of the stool upon which AI's future stability rests. Their interactions will determine whether the AI era produces resilience, equity, and innovation, or division, inequity, and mistrust.

Governments are the first leg of this triad, holding the formal authority to establish boundaries and protections. The European Union's AI Act is the clearest example of this role, setting risk-based classifications for AI applications and requiring transparency, oversight, and human accountability for high-risk systems (europa.eu). This legislation does more than regulate-it signals to the world that democratic governments can codify trust into law. In the U.S., the NIST AI Risk Management Framework offers a parallel approach, emphasizing reliability, accountability, and human-centered design as federal agencies and industry partners adopt AI (nist.gov).

Brookings notes that governments must strike a delicate balance: they must protect citizens from harm while enabling innovation that drives economic growth (brookings.edu). WHO adds another layer, stressing that in sectors like healthcare, global cooperation among governments is essential to prevent inequitable access and safety risks (who.int). Without government intervention, vulnerable communities risk being left behind or exploited. With too heavy a hand, governments may stifle innovation. The task is not easy, but it is unavoidable: governments must be both guardians of rights and enablers of progress.

But governments cannot do this work alone, and here the second leg of the triad-industry coalitions-emerges with equal weight. If governments write the rules, industry often builds the playing field. Technical standards, interoperability agreements, and infrastructure investments come largely from industry leaders. McKinsey reports that 70% of global firms experimenting with AI believe coalition-driven standards are more effective than unilateral regulation, as industry-led agreements often move faster and adapt more readily than legislative processes (mckinsey.com).

Gartner reinforces this by noting that coalitions across industries-finance, healthcare, education, and logistics-are increasingly essential to avoiding "AI silos" where systems cannot talk to one another (gartner.com). For example, credential verification in education must align with workforce recognition systems, and healthcare AI tools must integrate across borders and providers. Industry coalitions that share protocols and technologies create the connective tissue of a global AI economy.

Yet Brookings warns that leaving governance solely in industry hands risks subordinating public good to private profit. The EU's AI Act, in part, emerged as a response to unchecked industry dominance. Coalitions must therefore operate in tandem with governments and civil society, ensuring interoperability and investment do not outpace ethics. When industry coalitions prioritize not only efficiency but equity, they create the conditions for AI to scale responsibly.

The final leg of the triad-civil society networks-ensures that both governments and industries remain accountable to the people they serve. Grassroots coalitions, NGOs, universities, and advocacy groups bring ethical clarity and accountability to the governance conversation. UNESCO has emphasized that civil society's inclusion is essential to ensuring that marginalized voices shape AI frameworks, not just powerful governments and corporations (unesco.org).

Civil society is where lived realities meet governance. For example, WHO has pointed out that local advocacy groups in low- and middle-income countries are often the first to highlight inequities caused by health technologies, including AI (who.int). Their insights reveal blind spots in global governance and ensure that frameworks do not simply reflect the interests of elites. Brookings underscores that civil society also plays a trust-building role: citizens are more likely to accept AI systems when they see advocacy groups and universities involved in shaping safeguards (brookings.edu). These networks bring legitimacy from the ground up, balancing the top-down power of governments and the market-driven agendas of industry.

In the governance triad, civil society is not ornamental. It is the conscience. Without it, AI governance risks drifting into technocracy or plutocracy. With it, governance remains anchored in human dignity, rights, and justice. Civil society ensures that the governance triad reflects not only power but people. The most effective models will keep these three in dynamic tension: each strong enough to check the others, none dominant enough to dictate unilaterally.

From Compliance to Co-Design

One of the great failings of past technological governance was the tendency to treat regulation as an after-the-fact compliance checklist-something to be satisfied once innovation had already been deployed at scale, often after harms were discovered. With AI, we have a chance to do better, not by retrofitting accountability, but by embedding it from the beginning. Gartner has called this shift a move from "compliance-first" to "trust-by-design," urging that ethical and human-centered safeguards must be woven into the earliest stages of development rather than patched in later (gartner.com). In my view, this means creating systems where communities, policymakers, and industries do not simply react to AI, but actively co-design its trajectory. As we attempt furthering risk mitigation and advancement simultaneously, we must sweep ideas broadly across many intelligent domains, persons, states, and nations.

The first requirement of co-design is meaningful engagement at the front end. Education, workforce, policy, technology, and citizen voices must be present at the inception of AI systems, not invited in once systems are fully formed. Brookings has argued that such multistakeholder governance models improve legitimacy and accelerate adoption, because communities are more likely to trust technologies they have helped to shape (brookings.edu). In Tennessee, for example, our work at Motlow State and across the TBR system demonstrates how workforce leaders and educators together can define the competencies that AI-driven credentialing platforms must validate. Without their input, systems risk creating certificates of limited value in the labor market.

The WHO underscores this in healthcare: AI diagnostic systems must be developed with the input of clinicians, patients, and public health officials to avoid reinforcing inequities or missing cultural and contextual nuances (who.int). Similarly, the EU's AI Act enshrines consultation as part of its governance framework, ensuring that stakeholders, not just developers, influence how risk is classified and mitigated (europa.eu). In both global and local contexts, the lesson is clear-legitimacy and trust cannot be engineered in isolation. They must be co-created.

Use the iterative feedback loops to adapt governance as technology evolves. The second requirement of co-design is iteration. AI does not stand still; models evolve, data shifts, and use cases proliferate. Governance must evolve alongside them. In Volume I, I described the OODA framework-Observe, Orient, Decide, Act-as a way to keep governance dynamic. This iterative approach echoes McKinsey's finding that organizations embedding continuous governance loops are more likely to report successful AI scaling across multiple functions (mckinsey.com).

Feedback loops must be institutionalized, not improvised. Gartner notes that iterative oversight reduces systemic risk, particularly when failures are anticipated, reported, and corrected quickly (gartner.com). In Tennessee, the Motlow AI Literacy Survey of 2025 offered precisely such a loop: students, faculty, and staff provided feedback on pilot AI deployments, and those results directly shaped institutional decisions on training and support. At the global level, UNESCO's Recommendation on the Ethics of AI stresses the need for continual reassessment to ensure that governance remains relevant as contexts and technologies shift (unesco.org).

Iteration does more than manage risk-it builds resilience. WHO emphasizes that in health systems, iterative governance can prevent widespread harm by catching bias or safety issues early. Applied to education and workforce development, the same principle ensures that AI tools remain effective, equitable, and aligned with human dignity even as conditions change. Co-design, therefore, is not a one-time consultation but a continuous covenant.

We must ensure that trust-building is embedded at the design stage, not bolted on later. Moreover, we must co-design a means of embedding trust from the first line of code. Too often, trust is treated as a veneer-a set of assurances layered on top of systems after launch. But trust cannot be retrofitted. It must be structural. NIST's AI Risk Management Framework emphasizes that safety, explainability, and accountability must be designed into AI systems from the start, rather than appended as compliance requirements (nist.gov).

Embedding trust at design stage requires prioritizing transparency, fairness, and accountability as design requirements equal to performance or efficiency.

The EU's European Digital Identity Wallet pilot demonstrates this principle: trust protocols were foundational, ensuring portability and sovereignty were built in rather than added later (ec.europa.eu). McKinsey reinforces this point, showing that organizations prioritizing trust-by-design practices report 30-40% faster adoption rates than those that attempt to retrofit governance afterward (mckinsey.com).

Trust-by-design is more than a regulatory strategy; it is a philosophical stance. It acknowledges that AI systems are not neutral-they carry human values, assumptions, and biases. By embedding trust early, we acknowledge responsibility for those values and orient systems toward dignity, creativity, and fairness. UNESCO captures this best when it insists that the ethics of AI are not external to design but intrinsic to it. If we take this seriously, co-design becomes not only a technical practice but a humanistic imperative. Brookings emphasizes that early co-design reduces systemic risk and accelerates adoption by giving communities confidence in both process and outcome.

This next month, year, and decade matters. Technology's growth curve is not waiting for us. The next ten years will bring advances that once seemed speculative but are now on the cusp of widespread adoption. The urgency of governance comes from this accelerating timeline: decisions deferred today will calcify into structures, norms, and inequities by 2035. This is why foresight must become practice. Foresight … the changes are here cross-sector. We have humanoid integration into healthcare, logistics, and customer service.

Humanoid robotics are already entering pilot phases in healthcare, logistics, and service industries. The World Health Organization has noted that AI-driven robotics could help address critical shortages in elder care, clinical support, and rehabilitation services, particularly as global populations age (who.int). Yet WHO warns of significant risks: without safeguards, these systems could compromise dignity, reduce human-to-human interaction, and exacerbate inequities in access to quality care. For instance, robotics deployed in high-income nations may improve service delivery, while under-resourced regions are left with outdated or absent technologies.

McKinsey projects that humanoid robotics, integrated with AI, could automate 25-30% of repetitive tasks in logistics and healthcare by 2035, potentially adding trillions in productivity gains globally (mckinsey.com). But Brookings has cautioned that efficiency gains alone are not enough; what matters is whether automation augments human workers or displaces them (brookings.edu). For Tennessee and similar regions, humanoid integration must be framed as augmentation: tools that support nurses, caregivers, and frontline service staff, not replacements for their labor or empathy.

The governance imperative is therefore twofold: embed dignity safeguards into design-ensuring that humanoids reinforce care rather than diminish it-and ensure equitable access across geographies. UNESCO has emphasized that technologies affecting fundamental human experiences, like care, must be designed around human rights principles (unesco.org). Humanoid robotics will not simply test engineering; they will test our commitment to humanism in the age of machines. These commitments will also see us leverage both spatial and quantum computing today and into the future.

Spatial computing-the blending of physical and digital environments into immersive, interactive experiences-is poised to transform education, workforce training, and global collaboration. Gartner forecasts that by 2030, over half of enterprise design and training activities will involve spatial computing platforms, from virtual reality to augmented digital twins (gartner.com). These environments will allow learners in Tennessee to collaborate in real-time with peers in Nairobi or Berlin, breaking down geographic barriers to knowledge exchange.

In education, spatial computing can create immersive classrooms that respond to emotional cues and adapt to different learning styles. Brookings highlights that immersive technologies can foster deeper engagement and problem-solving, but warns that inequitable access to broadband and devices could create new divides (brookings.edu). For rural communities, including much of Tennessee's TBR service area, this raises immediate policy questions about infrastructure investment and digital equity.

The EU has already invested heavily in cross-border spatial computing collaborations, framing them as key to Europe's Digital Decade strategy (ec.europa.eu). UNESCO has similarly encouraged nations to view immersive technologies not only as pedagogical tools but as cultural preservation platforms, enabling communities to archive and share traditions in new formats. The governance question is clear: will spatial computing extend opportunity and culture across borders, or deepen divides between those with access and those without? This decade will decide.

Quantum computing represents perhaps the most disruptive force of all. Unlike incremental gains in processing, quantum breakthroughs will fundamentally upend how we encrypt, model, and accelerate AI systems. The

EU's Quantum Flagship anticipates major breakthroughs before 2035, particularly in breaking traditional encryption standards and accelerating simulation capacities for science and medicine (ec.europa.eu). Such breakthroughs will not just improve existing systems; they will render some current systems obsolete overnight.

WHO has raised concerns that without global governance, quantum-accelerated health AI could exacerbate inequities, delivering precision medicine in wealthy nations while leaving others with outdated methods. McKinsey estimates that quantum computing could contribute up to $1 trillion annually to the global economy by 2035, primarily through breakthroughs in pharmaceuticals, logistics, and climate modeling (mckinsey.com). Yet Gartner has warned that quantum computing also introduces existential risks: current encryption protocols protecting global financial and health systems could be broken, exposing massive vulnerabilities (gartner.com).

Brookings frames the challenge as one of foresight: if governance waits until quantum capacity arrives, the risks will already be embedded in our systems (brookings.edu). UNESCO emphasizes that trust in the quantum era will depend on transparent agreements about security, sovereignty, and equitable access. For Tennessee and for the U.S., this means embedding quantum literacy and governance frameworks into education and workforce planning now, ensuring that when the breakthroughs arrive, our communities are prepared not only to adopt but to shape the new order.

If we do not set robust governance norms before these technologies become widespread, we will find ourselves racing to regulate after harm has already been done. McKinsey estimates that regulatory lag could cost the global economy $2-3 trillion in unrealized productivity by 2035.

A Call to the Table: From Tennessee to the Global Assurances

Verification systems-credentialing, identity assurance, and AI risk classification-are not abstract technicalities; they are the trust rails upon which the next decade of education and workforce development will run. They must operate across layers: state by state, region by region, nationally, and ultimately internationally. Each level carries both promise and peril. If designed with foresight, verification systems can become bridges of equity and opportunity. If designed poorly, they risk becoming walls of exclusion or tools of surveillance.

At the state level, Tennessee offers a compelling case study. Within the Tennessee Board of Regents system, community colleges and technical colleges already serve more than 100,000 learners annually (tbr.edu), with the majority of these students being first-generation, Pell-eligible, and balancing work while in school. The Tennessee Higher Education Commission's 2024 Fact Book shows that over 70% of community college students in Tennessee work while enrolled (tn.gov/thec).

Verification systems here must capture not only traditional degrees but also micro-credentials, industry-recognized certifications, and experiential learning. The positive is agility: Tennessee has piloted blockchain-verified micro-credentials in advanced manufacturing and health sciences, aligning directly with regional workforce needs. The risk, however, is fragmentation. If credential schemas differ across institutions or states, a welding certificate in Tennessee may not be easily portable to Kentucky or North Carolina, limiting student mobility and employer recognition.

At the regional level, multi-state agreements could scale what Tennessee has pioneered. For example, regional verification frameworks across the Southeast could allow for portability of credentials in high-demand fields like healthcare, IT, and advanced manufacturing-all areas where the Tennessee Department of Labor projects steady or accelerated growth through 2030 (tn.gov/workforce). The positive outcome here is increased labor mobility across state lines, supporting industries like logistics in Memphis or healthcare in Nashville that draw workers regionally. The risk, however, is inequity: smaller colleges or underfunded states may struggle to meet technical standards, leaving certain learners disadvantaged. Gartner warns that regional coalitions without equity mechanisms risk creating tiers of trustworthiness, where some credentials are recognized and others are not (gartner.com).
At the national level, verification systems can deliver consistency and legitimacy. The U.S. could align with NIST's AI Risk Management Framework (nist.gov) to establish nationwide standards for credential assurance, fairness audits, and data transparency. For Tennessee, this would mean that a credential earned at Motlow or Nashville State carries the same recognition and digital verification safeguards as one earned in California or New York. The positive is coherence: students would have portable skills across all 50 states, and employers would trust what they see. But the risk is rigidity. The WHO cautions that centralized systems often overlook local context, potentially imposing uniformity that fails to reflect unique workforce dynamics in places like rural Appalachia or Middle Tennessee (who.int).

At the international level, verification systems hold the greatest potential and the greatest risk. UNESCO's Recommendation on the Ethics of AI underscores that cross-border credential recognition is essential for global equity, particularly for migrants, refugees, and international learners (unesco.org). McKinsey estimates that portable, verifiable credentials could unlock hundreds of billions of dollars in labor mobility and productivity globally(mckinsey.com). For Tennessee, with growing international investment in advanced manufacturing (e.g., Nissan, Ultium Cells, Mitsubishi), internationally verifiable credentials would mean that local graduates could work seamlessly with global supply chains. Yet Brookings warns of the "sovereignty paradox": without strong safeguards, global verification risks becoming surveillance infrastructure, concentrating power in a few dominant systems (brookings.edu).

The way forward is layered trust. States like Tennessee innovate and adapt quickly; regions harmonize for mobility; nations standardize for legitimacy; and international frameworks harmonize principles without erasing sovereignty. The positives are compelling: greater student mobility, stronger employer confidence, and faster adoption of skills-based hiring. The risks are equally real: exclusion, rigidity, and the potential misuse of verification as a control mechanism rather than an empowerment tool. The test of this decade will be whether Tennessee-and the world-can design verification systems that act as bridges of trust and dignity, not gates of compliance.

It also demands that voices from the margins are present and heard. WHO and UNESCO have both stressed that equitable AI governance requires elevating voices from the Global South and historically marginalized communities, not just G7 or OECD states. Without their input, governance risks perpetuating the very inequities AI has the potential to reduce.

We began this journey by asking how AI could transform our systems of teaching, innovation, and work. We now find ourselves asking how those systems can transform AI-shaping it into a trusted, equitable, and globally coherent tool for human advancement. The answer will not come from a single policy or a single nation. It will come from the network of relationships we choose to build - relationships strong enough to carry both trust and technology into the future.

References - Chapter 4

1. World Health Organization. Ethics and Governance of Artificial Intelligence for Health. who.int

2. McKinsey & Company. The State of AI in 2024. mckinsey.com

3. Gartner. AI Governance Survey 2023; Trust-by-Design Recommendations. gartner.com

4. European Union. The AI Act. europa.eu

5. European Commission. European Digital Identity Wallet Pilot. europa.eu

6. UNESCO. Recommendation on the Ethics of Artificial Intelligence. unesco.org

7. National Institute of Standards and Technology. AI Risk Management Framework. nist.gov

8. Brookings Institution. Making AI Work for Schools; Creative Patterns in the Age of AI; Global AI Governance. brookings.edu

9. Gartner. AI Governance Survey 2023; Digital Trust in AI Adoption. gartner.com

10. European Commission. Digital Compass 2030 and European Digital Strategy. ec.europa.eu

11. Brookings Institution. Global AI Governance: Balancing Standards and Sovereignty. brookings.edu

12. Gartner. AI Governance Survey 2023; Interoperability Risks in AI. gartner.com

13. National Institute of Standards and Technology. AI Risk Management Framework. nist.gov

14. Brookings Institution. Global AI Governance: Balancing Standards and Sovereignty; AI and the Workforce. brookings.edu

15. Gartner. AI Governance Survey 2023; Future of Spatial Computing and Quantum Risk. gartner.com

16. European Union. AI Act; Quantum Flagship Program; Digital Decade Strategy. europa.eu; ec.europa.eu

17. Tennessee Board of Regents (TBR). Fast Facts and System Reports 2024-2025. tbr.edu

18. Tennessee Higher Education Commission (THEC). Tennessee Higher Education Fact Book 2024-2025. tn.gov/thec

19. Tennessee Department of Labor & Workforce Development. Occupational Projections and Labor Market Information. tn.gov/workforce

20. UNESCO. Recommendation on the Ethics of AI. unesco.org

21. European Commission. European Digital Identity Wallet; Digital Decade Strategy. ec.europa.eu

22. McKinsey & Company. State of AI in 2024; Cross-Border Labor Mobility Analysis. mckinsey.com

23. Brookings Institution. Global AI Governance and Mobility Research. brookings.edu

Chapter 5 - Universally Integrated Systems for Education and Workforce

In Volume I, we defined the Universally Integrated System (UIS) as a vision for linking disparate platforms - K-12, higher education, industry, and government - into a seamless network where skills, credentials, and employment opportunities flow in real time. At the time, UIS was a disruptive idea for Tennessee and the surrounding region. Now, it is no longer just an innovation - it is an imperative, but it begs the question around centralized and decentralized ownership models. This is a discussion for a later date. Further, the reason is simple and moving, talent mobility has gone global, and our systems for developing and recognizing talent have not kept pace. The journey of being the best state in the best nation means one thing to get there, it is quite more than strategy, but tactical intentionality to stay atop and remain dominant. A UIS is no longer optional.

For example, today, a credential earned in Murfreesboro might need to be verified by an employer in Munich or recognized by a licensing authority in Japan, South Korea, or Nairobi. Without interoperable systems, learners spend weeks proving skills they already have, employers face delays and uncertainty in hiring across borders, and governments lose the ability to track workforce readiness in real time. Is it possible to create a labor force consortium that not only pulls from the UIS, but also taps the seemingly qualified based on durable skill identification and other caveats, to advantage Tennesseans or other global citizens? The absence of a UIS at scale creates friction that disadvantages learners, slows business innovation, and leaves entire sectors underprepared for rapid economic shifts, perhaps even more so in rural communities.

What core principles are necessary for UIS. To function across geographies and sectors, a Universal Interoperability System (UIS) must be guided by three essential principles. The first is interoperability by design. Credentials, transcripts, and skills profiles must be portable and verifiable across platforms, jurisdictions, and industries. In Tennessee, blockchain pilots in advanced manufacturing and healthcare programs have already shown that a credential can be verified in seconds by an employer. The positive here is speed and trust: employers know the credential source, and learners see immediate value. The risk, however, is that if interoperability standards are not carefully aligned, systems become fragmented or too rigid, either undermining portability or erasing local nuance. Colorado's Education Exchange pilot and Texas's Tri-Agency Workforce Initiative are proof that interoperability can be designed into statewide systems while still respecting local contexts.

The second principle is agency and privacy for the learner. THEC data shows that 70% of Tennessee community college students work while enrolled, often needing to demonstrate specific competencies to employers before completing full degrees. UIS must give them the ability to share selected credentials without exposing entire academic records. UNESCO has stressed that student sovereignty over data is not optional but foundational to dignity. In New York, SUNY's microcredentialing initiative demonstrates how learner-controlled wallets protect agency while ensuring verifiability. The risk, of course, lies in surveillance creep-if UIS is designed without robust consent mechanisms, it could become another system of extraction rather than empowerment.

The third principle is cultural and economic relevance. Credentials must balance global alignment with local fidelity. A welding certificate in Tennessee should carry baseline competencies comparable to one in Tokyo, but it should also reflect Tennessee's specific economic context-such as advanced manufacturing and automotive supply chains. The Tennessee Department of Labor projects sustained demand in these fields through 2030, meaning UIS must ensure credentials align with these realities (tn.gov/workforce). Texas has aligned welding standards with petrochemical industries, while Colorado has tied them to renewable energy and aerospace. This shows how modular taxonomies allow regions to add competencies without breaking interoperability. Brookings reminds us that frameworks must align "without erasure," so that local expertise is not devalued in a credential monoculture.

Together, these three principles-interoperability, agency, and cultural relevance-are the architecture of trust in UIS. They transform records into bridges of equity, linking learners, employers, and communities across boundaries. Without them, UIS risks becoming another bureaucratic layer. With them, it becomes a dynamic trust fabric capable of carrying both technology and dignity into the future.

Our Metaversity project served as a first-generation prototype of UIS. The blockchain-secured digital wallet carried skills, credentials, and experiences that were portable across devices, available on demand, and linked to live job boards. In Tennessee, this meant a mechatronics student could present verifiable competencies to an employer like Nissan instantly. What we imagined was a local proof of concept; what we realized was a glimpse into a global future. In a fully developed UIS, that same Tennessee student could apply for a position in Germany, with the credential instantly recognized by HR and verified by the relevant trade authority.

Colorado has tested similar concepts with its Education Exchange, which links K-12, higher education, and workforce records in a unified blockchain-based platform. Texas has experimented with blockchain verification in healthcare credentials, while New York's SUNY system has piloted industry-linked digital microcredentials. Each state provides a laboratory for scaling UIS. What made Tennessee's Metaversity unique was its direct integration with live employer systems, closing the loop between education and employment in real time. The lesson is clear: UIS is not only about digital wallets-it is about building trust loops across sectors.

The risks of scaling are significant. Gartner warns that over 60% of credentialing platforms fail to scale regionally or nationally because interoperability is not embedded at design. Without policy harmonization, UIS can devolve into siloed experiments that don't translate across borders. Yet the positives are powerful: reduced friction in hiring, improved student confidence, and faster workforce alignment. In Tennessee, employers reported shorter hiring times when blockchain-verified credentials were piloted, and learners valued the immediacy of recognition.

Metaversity taught us that UIS is not hypothetical-it is possible, here and now. The challenge is not invention but expansion: aligning technologies, policies, and governance so that local prototypes become global systems of trust. The need for a continuation of active policy development will be key.

Technology alone will not scale UIS; it must be embedded in policy infrastructure. At the local level, agreements between schools, colleges, and employers must map curricula to verified skill taxonomies. TBR has long partnered with industry-from automotive giants to regional hospitals-to align programs with workforce needs.

Colorado's Career Pathways Framework and Texas's tri-agency partnerships provide similar local-to-employer pipelines. The benefit is agility: curricula can adapt to labor demand quickly. The risk is fragmentation-if local systems are not interoperable, learners and employers lose portability beyond their communities.

At the national level, mutual recognition frameworks ensure consistency. Texas' statewide integration across education and workforce shows how one state can build coherence internally. New York's SUNY system has coordinated microcredential recognition across campuses, making employer interpretation consistent. For Tennessee, UIS could align with NIST's AI Risk

Management Framework, ensuring credentials are trusted nationally for fairness, reliability, and security. McKinsey emphasizes that national coherence accelerates scaling and reduces redundancy, but warns of rigidity if innovation is stifled.

At the global level, UIS requires cross-border agreements on verification standards, privacy, and data exchange. UNESCO's ethical framework and the EU's AI Act both call for shared principles of portability, accountability, and consent. WHO highlights that global health AI cannot succeed without interoperable standards that prevent inequitable outcomes. Sovereignty is the risk: nations may resist alignment to protect local control. But the opportunity is transformative: UIS can become the backbone of a global workforce economy, connecting learners and employers across continents.

Policy is the glue that binds technology to legitimacy. Without it, UIS will remain a patchwork of local pilots. With it, UIS can scale from Tennessee to the world, enabling learners and employers to trust one another across borders. In my work, this is where I can see scalable optimization.

A mature UIS must go beyond static record-keeping; it must function as an active intelligence network. Tennessee's labor market data projects rising demand in cybersecurity, advanced manufacturing, and healthcare-fields where skill gaps could quickly undermine growth. UIS should be able to flag these gaps, suggest microcredentials to learners in real time, and track progress continuously. For a working student in Shelbyville, this could mean receiving an automated recommendation for a cybersecurity credential tied directly to local employer demand.

Colorado is already testing predictive analytics for workforce pipelines, and Texas is piloting real-time dashboards that connect credentials to employer needs. In New York, SUNY campuses are working with industry partners to embed skill feedback loops directly into curricula. These models show how UIS can move education from reactive to anticipatory-preparing people for tomorrow's jobs before they even appear on postings.

McKinsey estimates that real-time alignment could reduce workforce mismatches by 20% globally, saving billions in lost productivity. Brookings argues that anticipatory systems particularly benefit marginalized learners, who often lack early access to labor market signals. The risk, however, is misuse: if predictive analytics are poorly governed, they may reinforce bias by channeling learners into narrow pathways. WHO and UNESCO both insist that equity and dignity safeguards must accompany predictive alignment.

Tennessee's own pilots suggest the power of this approach. When we linked employer demand data to credential dashboards, employers reported faster hiring and students reported greater clarity about pathways. A global UIS could deliver that same advantage-anticipating skill needs, empowering learners, and accelerating opportunity at scale. We need not be cautious, but we need to be risk adverse and aware of the guardrails necessary.

Scaling UIS globally carries a real risk: the erosion of local learning cultures. If over-standardized, UIS could create a credential monoculture where unique expertise and cultural nuance are undervalued. Tennessee's whiskey distilling programs, for example, require competencies specific to local industries that cannot be captured in a generic global taxonomy.

To prevent this, UIS must include metadata layers that capture cultural, economic, and linguistic context. Modular skill frameworks should allow local competencies to be added without breaking global interoperability. Brookings has argued that modularity is essential for equity-without it, smaller or non-dominant cultures risk erasure. Colorado's renewable energy pathways and Texas's petrochemical credentials demonstrate how local specializations must be preserved even within standardized systems.

UNESCO emphasizes that cultural identity is a form of human dignity, and UIS must encode it alongside global competencies. WHO echoes this in healthcare: diagnostic models must reflect local disease burdens and contexts to remain accurate. Over-standardization is efficient but brittle; modularity is messy but resilient.

The goal is alignment without erasure. UIS must be capable of speaking a global language while respecting local dialects. In Tennessee, this means welding and mechatronics align with global standards but retain regional distinctives. Globally, it means a UIS that values not only efficiency but humanity.

Scaling UIS requires coalitions that can cross boundaries of sector and nation. Education coalitions must align curriculum standards with shared skill frameworks. Industry coalitions must update those frameworks in real time as technologies evolve. Government coalitions must build the regulatory backbone for recognition and privacy.

Colorado's UIS pilots succeeded because state agencies, universities, and employers worked together. Texas' tri-agency approach-linking higher education, workforce, and K-12-demonstrates how governance alignment accelerates scaling. New York's SUNY partnerships with healthcare and IT industries show the necessity of employer validation. In Tennessee, our coalition of TBR institutions, industry partners, and local governments has proven that multisector collaboration builds trust.

McKinsey and Gartner both argue that coalition-driven standards scale faster and carry more legitimacy than unilateral efforts. Brookings calls them "living governance"-frameworks that evolve as coalitions update them, rather than ossifying on decade-long cycles. UNESCO insists that marginalized voices must be included, or coalitions will simply reproduce inequities. The risk is tokenism; the opportunity is legitimacy.

Coalitions that count are not ceremonial-they are functional. They do the hard work of drafting, implementing, and enforcing standards in real time. UIS will live or die on the strength of these coalitions. The road ahead looks open and inviting, from the hollers-n-hills, mountains to seas, and across oceans and hemispheres. We can accomplish this together and we already have examples.

Our regional UIS work in Tennessee has already shown promise. Completion rates rise when students see their verified skills in real time. Employers hire faster when they trust the source of credentials. Policymakers make better funding decisions when workforce readiness data is current and comprehensive. These lessons echo those in Colorado, Texas, and New York, where regional pilots have produced measurable gains in efficiency and trust.

The next challenge is scale. Building a UIS that operates across counties is a start. Building one that operates across continents is the task of the decade. WHO reminds us that global health inequities demand interoperable solutions. UNESCO insists that international mobility requires dignity-preserving verification. McKinsey calculates that the cost of delay is measured in trillions.

The risks are real: exclusion, rigidity, and surveillance creep. But the positives are greater: a UIS that moves as easily between continents as it does between counties, carrying learners, workers, and communities into the future. Tennessee has laid a foundation. Now we must join with Colorado, Texas, New York, and global partners to build the trust architecture of a connected, equitable workforce.

The road ahead is not only about technology. It is about trust, coalition, and human dignity. UIS, if built wisely, can become the backbone of a truly global, truly equitable workforce system. That is not only possible; it is necessary.

References - Chapter 5

1. Tennessee Board of Regents (TBR). Fast Facts and System Reports 2024-2025. tbr.edu

2. Tennessee Higher Education Commission (THEC). Tennessee Higher Education Fact Book 2024-2025. tn.gov/thec

3. Tennessee Department of Labor & Workforce Development. Occupational Projections and Labor Market Information. tn.gov/workforce

4. Colorado Department of Higher Education. Colorado Education Exchange Pilot; Career Pathways Framework.highered. colorado.gov

5. Texas Higher Education Coordinating Board / Tri-Agency Workforce Initiative. Building a Talent Strong Texas. highered.texas.gov

6. State University of New York (SUNY). Microcredentials at SUNY. suny.edu

7. European Commission. Artificial Intelligence Act; European Digital Identity Wallet; Digital Decade Strategy. europa.eu; ec.europa.eu

8. National Institute of Standards and Technology (NIST). AI Risk Management Framework. nist.gov

9. World Health Organization (WHO). Ethics and Governance of Artificial Intelligence for Health. who.int

10. UNESCO. Recommendation on the Ethics of Artificial Intelligence. unesco.org

11. McKinsey & Company. The State of AI in 2024; The Future of Work

and Skills Alignment. mckinsey.com

12. Brookings Institution. Global AI Governance: Balancing Standards and Sovereignty; AI and the Workforce; Align Without Erasure. brookings.edu

13. Gartner AI Governance Survey 2023; Trust-by-Design Recommendations; Interoperability Risks in AI Systems. gartner.com

Chapter 6 - Skills, Competencies, and the New Lexicon of Work

The language of work is changing faster than the systems we use to recognize it. Once, a résumé sufficed. Then came transcripts, diplomas, and certifications. Today, we confront a growing lexicon of micro-credentials, skill assertions, badges, and blockchain-verified profiles - signals in a labor market where learning can happen anywhere, anytime, and must be proven on demand. Tennessee's pilots in blockchain verification within TBR have shown us both the promise and the complexity of this transition. Learners carry portable credentials, but employers still struggle to interpret them consistently. This tension is not unique to Tennessee; Colorado's workforce data pilots, Texas's tri-agency alignment, and New York's SUNY system all reveal the same need: a new lexicon for a new era of work. Do we start with begging the questions, "Who can credential?"

Today, nearly anyone can issue a credential: universities, industry associations, unions, employers, ed-tech firms, even individual instructors. This democratization has value - it expands recognition to diverse forms of learning. But it also creates risk. The Tennessee Higher Education Commission's 2024 Fact Book shows that more than 40% of learners in community colleges pursue non-degree credentials, yet employers often question their rigor. Credential inflation becomes inevitable when a "badge" for a one-hour webinar looks, at least superficially, like a competency-based industry certification. Brookings has warned that without transparent, auditable accreditation of credential issuers, credibility erodes (brookings.edu).

Colorado has begun addressing this through its Credential Quality Framework, auditing providers for rigor and impact. Texas, via the Tri-Agency Workforce Initiative, requires mapping credentials to labor demand, while New York's SUNY system embeds employer review into micro-credential approvals. Globally, UNESCO and NIST stress the need for transparent registries of credential issuers (unesco.org; nist.gov). A universal registry would allow learners and employers alike to verify not only the credential but the credibility of its issuer. The opportunity here is accountability; the risk is opacity.

A sustainable future requires credentialing bodies that are themselves transparent, subject to independent audits, and mapped against global standards. Tennessee can lead by combining our blockchain pilots with an open state registry verified by THEC and the Department of Labor. That model, scaled nationally, would reduce inflation, preserve legitimacy, and give learners confidence that their efforts will be recognized. Moreover, it will drive the response to counting credentials.

The traditional boundaries between academic and vocational, degree and certification, are dissolving. A 16-year-old in Murfreesboro completing a robotics credential may be more job-ready than a mechanical engineering graduate elsewhere. Tennessee Department of Labor projections confirm that sub-baccalaureate technical credentials are in highest demand statewide. McKinsey reports similar trends globally: employers prioritize specific, verifiable competencies over degrees in many sectors (mckinsey.com).

Defining what counts requires three commitments: first, global skill taxonomies so competencies align across borders; second, evidence-based assertion so every credential ties to demonstrable performance, not attendance; third, contextual relevance so credentials reflect both universal baselines and local realities. Colorado's renewable energy frameworks, Texas's petrochemical training, and SUNY's IT microcredentials all illustrate local inflections of global competencies.

Brookings argues that skill taxonomies are the lingua franca of mobility, and UNESCO stresses the need to encode local context into global frameworks. For Tennessee, this means ensuring that welding or health sciences credentials map onto international frameworks but still encode the regional context - from OSHA codes to local hospital standards. The positive here is portability; the risk is homogenization.

UIS, as described in Chapter 4, becomes the infrastructure for translating credentials into globally recognized yet locally meaningful signals. What counts must be defined collaboratively - with equity, rigor, and context at the center.

Assertion in the Age of AI and Blockchain lights up the circuits. Assertion has shifted from personal claim to machine-mediated verification. In the analog era, "I can do this" was backed by reputation or interview. Today, AI matches wallet-based skills to job requirements, and blockchain verifies authenticity of the issuing body. The EU's Digital Wallet and Tennessee's blockchain pilots both show the power of instant verification. But assertion without context can mislead. A U.S. credential in "data analytics" may not align with regulatory or business practices in India or Brazil.

Metadata layers are essential. UNESCO emphasizes that credentials must carry scope, limitations, and contextual markers, ensuring assertions are meaningful globally. NIST's AI Risk Management Framework supports contextualization as part of trustworthy design. Without these layers, assertion risks becoming noise. With them, it becomes a global signal of capability.

Colorado and Texas are testing metadata-rich credential frameworks tied to labor market demand. New York is piloting blockchain verification with contextual data fields. Tennessee can expand Metaversity wallets to include contextual tags, ensuring that every credential is not just valid but interpretable across geographies.

The stewardship challenge remains: ensuring AI verification and blockchain authentication don't outpace human understanding. Assertion must remain interpretable, credible, and situated in real-world application. From possession to performance, the future of work demands proof of performance, not possession of credentials alone. Digital portfolios linking microcredentials to project evidence are already appearing in SUNY and Colorado pilots. Simulation-based assessments are emerging in Texas's health sciences and aviation programs. In Tennessee, TBR's mechatronics training increasingly relies on simulation and competency demonstrations.

McKinsey projects that performance-based verification could reduce skill mismatches by up to 20% globally. Gartner reports that simulation and continuous assessment cycles are rapidly becoming employer-preferred (gartner.com). But risks exist. WHO warns that performance-based AI assessments must be carefully audited for bias, lest they exclude learners from marginalized groups.

UIS integration strengthens performance-based systems: AI can monitor credential "expiration" as technologies evolve, prompting learners toward upskilling before obsolescence. Tennessee pilots could embed such continuous monitoring in fields like cybersecurity, where rapid skill decay is a known risk. Performance transforms credentials into living documents - evidence not of past possession but current capability. It shifts the focus from seat time to proven mastery, aligning perfectly with employer demand and learner needs.

The role of employers and industry coalitions is alive and well in states like Tennessee and others. Employers must move from passive consumers to active co-creators of credentials. Tennessee partnerships with Nissan, Mitsubishi, and Ultium Cells have shown the power of co-design. Competencies are benchmarked against real-world requirements, then embedded in curriculum. Colorado's renewable energy industry, Texas's oil and gas sector, and New York's finance and healthcare hubs are doing the same.

Industry coalitions must also ensure standards travel across borders. A Tennessee welding certificate should map onto frameworks recognized in São Paulo or Munich. Brookings emphasizes that cross-border industry coalitions reduce skill gaps and enhance economic integration. UNESCO reinforces that global frameworks must include diverse economic contexts, not just dominant economies.

The risk is employer dominance skewing frameworks toward narrow corporate interests. The positive is responsiveness, legitimacy, and alignment with workforce demand. McKinsey highlights that coalition-led standards scale faster than government mandates alone. UIS provides connective tissue. Employers embed requirements, educators align curricula, and learners carry globally interpretable credentials. This is the coalition model that works with equity in the "New Lexicon." The new lexicon carries risks of exclusion. If verification tools remain costly or inaccessible, marginalized learners are locked out. If lived experience is ignored, systems replicate inequities. THEC's data shows that rural Tennessee students and first-generation learners remain underrepresented in credential pipelines. Brookings warns that inequity in credentialing risks compounding existing divides.

Equity must mean free or low-cost verification, recognition of informal and community-based learning, and multiple pathways to earn credentials - from apprenticeship to project work. UNESCO stresses recognition of non-formal learning as key to equity. WHO underscores equity in health AI credentialing as essential for fair outcomes. Colorado has piloted equity-focused recognition frameworks, Texas has invested in apprenticeship-based credentialing, and New York has integrated community-based learning into SUNY microcredential design. Tennessee can continue this leadership by embedding lived experience recognition into UIS wallets. The risk is clear: privilege systems may accelerate opportunity gaps. The positive is equally clear: equity safeguards make UIS not just more just, but more effective in solving skill shortages.

From Local Trust to Global Recognition as the now of work continually shrinks the planet and access to broader gateways of employment, skill attainment, and credentialing proofs. UIS is the infrastructure; the lexicon is the currency. For this new currency to carry value, it must be portable across borders while retaining local nuance. That requires global recognition agreements backed by verifiable evidence and transparent governance.

McKinsey estimates that global mobility unlocked by credential portability could add hundreds of billions annually to productivity. Brookings warns that without recognition, skills remain stranded in local markets. Tennessee's welding certificate must be legible not just in Nashville but in Nagoya. Colorado, Texas, and New York show that alignment is possible when employer, government, and education coalitions work together.

The risk is homogenization; the opportunity is mobility. UNESCO insists that cultural specificity must remain embedded. WHO reminds us that portability in healthcare is life-critical. The EU's AI Act and Digital Wallet provide a usable template for global recognition. When recognition works, credentials stop being artifacts. They become living signals of capacity and credibility - not just locally, not just nationally, but globally.

References - Chapter 6

1. Tennessee Board of Regents (TBR). Fast Facts and System Reports 2024-2025. tbr.edu

2. Tennessee Higher Education Commission (THEC). Tennessee Higher Education Fact Book 2024-2025. tn.gov/thec

3. Tennessee Department of Labor & Workforce Development. Occupational Projections and Labor Market Information. tn.gov/workforce

4. Colorado Department of Higher Education. Credential Quality Framework; Colorado Education Exchange; Career Pathways Framework. highered.colorado.gov

5. Texas Higher Education Coordinating Board / Tri-Agency Workforce Initiative. Building a Talent Strong Texas; State Workforce Reports. highered.texas.gov

Chapter 7 - From OER to Adaptive Immersion: The Future of Open, AI-Enhanced Learning

When we first embraced Open Educational Resources (OER) at Motlow, the driver was simple: economic justice. Students were burdened by the high cost of textbooks. By adopting OER, we reduced costs and expanded access. Over time, OER evolved into more than a cost-saving tool. It became a platform for agility - the ability to remix curricula, respond to workforce needs, and engage learner interests more dynamically. Now, the next frontier is here: OER enhanced by adaptiveness, immersion, and intelligence.

The Shift from Static to Dynamic

Traditional OER remains largely static - PDFs, slide decks, recorded lectures. Useful, but limited. Adaptive OER must be dynamic: adjusting content in real time to learner pace and performance, offering AI-generated practice, and embedding immersive simulations. Gartner predicts that by 2030, over half of higher education learning materials will include adaptive components (gartner.com).

Tennessee pilots already show promise: in health sciences, simulation-based OER modules allow learners to practice clinical decisions. Colorado has piloted OER in renewable energy training with adaptive case studies. Texas has embedded AI-enhanced OER into workforce upskilling for manufacturing. New York has tied SUNY's OER programs directly to microcredential frameworks.

The benefit is responsiveness. The risk is inequity if adaptive OER requires expensive tools. UNESCO and Brookings stress that open content must remain accessible and inclusive. The shift is not just digital - it is philosophical. OER must move from static access to dynamic responsiveness.

AI as the Adaptive Engine

AI will be the engine of adaptive OER. It can reorder modules, generate personalized pathways, and translate content culturally and linguistically. NIST stresses the need for trustworthy AI design in education, ensuring personalization aligns with pedagogical goals. UNESCO echoes this, emphasizing cultural and linguistic adaptation as essential for equity.

Tennessee could build adaptive OER in automotive and advanced manufacturing, where students often juggle work and study. Colorado's adaptive OER in renewable energy demonstrates local-global relevance. Texas is piloting predictive OER interventions for students at risk of dropping out. New York's SUNY OER initiatives integrate employer-driven datasets to personalize pathways.

The opportunity is precision and equity; the risk is surveillance or bias if AI tools are unchecked. WHO insists adaptive learning must be inclusive and human-centered, with educators guiding AI rather than AI replacing them.

Immersive Learning Environments

Adaptive immersion extends learning into AR, VR, and spatial computing. Tennessee's AR welding labs and VR healthcare simulations already show the power of immersive OER. Colorado has piloted VR for aerospace training. Texas uses AR for manufacturing processes. New York has integrated VR nursing simulations into SUNY health sciences.

Gartner projects that immersive learning will become a core workforce pipeline strategy by 2035. Brookings argues that immersive OER democratizes access to advanced training once reserved for elite labs. The risk is cost - without open licensing, immersive tools could exacerbate inequity. UNESCO emphasizes the need for global commons to prevent commercial lock-in.

Immersion, when tied to openness, becomes a multiplier. An AR welding module from Tennessee could be adapted for Kenyan polytechnics. A VR nursing simulation from Singapore could be translated for Canadian students. This is the promise of adaptive OER: global reach with local fidelity.

OER in the UIS Ecosystem

UIS provides the infrastructure for credentialing and verification. Adaptive OER becomes the content layer, feeding UIS with verifiable learning outcomes.

Tennessee can link adaptive OER directly to credential wallets, ensuring employer-trusted verification. Colorado, Texas, and New York show how OER can flow into workforce dashboards, informing policy and funding decisions.

McKinsey estimates that OER linked to credential verification could reduce workforce mismatches by 15-20% globally. Brookings emphasizes that data-rich OER can improve policy by offering near-real-time insights into learner progression. The risk, however, is privacy. NIST and WHO insist that adaptive systems must minimize data collection and protect learner dignity.

UIS plus adaptive OER creates a continuous loop: learning → verification → workforce alignment. This is education redesigned for equity and agility.

Guardrails for the AI-OER Nexus

Guardrails are essential. Learners must know when AI has generated or modified content. Bias auditing must be routine, ensuring inclusivity. Data privacy must be sacrosanct. Without these, adaptive OER risks becoming exploitative. UNESCO and Brookings emphasize transparency, while NIST provides a framework for ethical AI deployment.

Tennessee can lead by embedding AI guardrails into adaptive OER design. Colorado and Texas have piloted equity audits for AI in education. SUNY requires public reporting of OER adaptations. WHO echoes the need for systematic auditing to avoid inequity.

The opportunity is enormous. The risk, unmanaged, is equally profound. Guardrails are not constraints; they are trust-builders.

From Access to Agency

The first wave of OER was about access. The next must be about agency. Learners should shape their learning experiences: choose modalities, integrate employer projects, and remix content. Educators should have the freedom to re-sequence materials in real time. Employers should embed real-world problems into adaptive OER.

Colorado, Texas, and New York pilots show that agency increases engagement and completion. THEC's Tennessee data demonstrates that students thrive when learning is flexible and contextual. McKinsey confirms that agency is a predictor of retention and workforce readiness.

Agency ties directly to UIS wallets and the credentialing lexicon of Chapter 6. It empowers learners to control not only credentials but also the pathways leading to them.

A Global Commons for Adaptive OER

Adaptive OER must be built as a global commons. Content repositories must be interoperable across languages and platforms. Development costs must be shared across nations and institutions. Policies must prevent commercial lock-in of publicly funded adaptive content.

UNESCO argues for open licensing as an ethical imperative. WHO stresses that healthcare training must be globally shareable. The EU's Digital Strategy points toward interoperable content frameworks. Brookings adds that shared commons reduce duplication and enhance equity.

In practice, an AR welding tutorial from Tennessee could be localized for Nairobi. A VR nursing simulation from SUNY could be adapted for Southeast Asia. A renewable energy case from Colorado could serve both Texas and Germany. This is what a commons can deliver.

The Road to Adaptive Immersion

We stand at a convergence. The credentialing system (Chapter 6) is becoming agile and performance-based. UIS (Chapter 4) is enabling global portability. Adaptive OER is preparing to deliver immersive, intelligent learning at scale. The next task is integration: uniting these into a seamless ecosystem. When UIS, credentials, and adaptive OER converge, the gap between learning and work closes.

1. Learners move from access to agency, from possession to performance, from local recognition to global mobility.

2. Employers hire with trust.

3. Policymakers invest with clarity.

4. Communities thrive with resilience.

This is not a distant vision. Tennessee, Colorado, Texas, and New York have already piloted the pieces. The challenge of this decade is to assemble them. The road ahead is one of coalition, design, and trust. With adaptive immersion, we are not only building a workforce for tomorrow - we are building a human-centered system of learning that honors dignity, equity, and opportunity across the globe.

References - Chapter 7

1. Tennessee Board of Regents (TBR). Fast Facts and System Reports 2024-2025. tbr.edu

2. Tennessee Higher Education Commission (THEC). Tennessee Higher Education Fact Book 2024-2025. tn.gov/thec

3. Tennessee Department of Labor & Workforce Development. Occupational Projections and Labor Market Information. tn.gov/workforce

4. Colorado Department of Higher Education. Credential Quality Framework; Colorado Education Exchange; Career Pathways Framework. highered.colorado.gov

5. Texas Higher Education Coordinating Board / Tri-Agency Workforce Initiative. Building a Talent Strong Texas; State Workforce Reports. highered.texas.gov

6. State University of New York (SUNY). Microcredentials at SUNY; SUNY OER Services. suny.edu

7. National Institute of Standards and Technology (NIST). AI Risk Management Framework. nist.gov

8. European Commission. Artificial Intelligence Act; European Digital Identity Wallet; Digital Decade Strategy. europa.eu; ec.europa.eu

9. World Health Organization (WHO). Ethics and Governance of Artificial Intelligence for Health. who.int

10. UNESCO. Recommendation on the Ethics of Artificial Intelligence; OER Commons Guidance. unesco.org

11. McKinsey & Company. The State of AI in 2024; The Future of Work and Skills Alignment. mckinsey.com

12. Brookings Institution Global AI Governance: Balancing Standards and Sovereignty; Skills and Workforce Policy; OER and Equity Reports. brookings.edu

13. Gartner. AI Governance Survey 2023; Trust-by-Design Recommendations; Future of Spatial Computing; Immersive Learning Trends. gartner.com

Chapter 8 - The Feedback Society: Continuous Learning and the OODA Loop

The OODA Loop - Observe, Orient, Decide, Act - has moved from a Cold War cockpit to the core of our learning ecosystems. Originally crafted by Colonel John Boyd for fighter pilots, its adaptability has carried it into entrepreneurship, healthcare, and education. In Volume I, we positioned OODA as a leadership compass; now, in this new decade, it has become the operating system for continuous improvement.

The "feedback society" is no longer speculative - it is emerging in classrooms, workplaces, and communities that refuse to wait for end-of-year reports or five-year labor studies. The challenge is whether we can design OODA-driven systems that enhance human flourishing, rather than overwhelm us with noise.

From Static Cycles to Perpetual Loops

Feedback once arrived too late to matter. A student saw their grades weeks after a test, a worker sat through an annual review, and policymakers pored over multi-year labor reports after opportunities had already shifted. In Tennessee, this model created a lag between what learners knew, what employers needed, and what communities could provide. In a feedback society, those cycles compress. Today, AI dashboards allow instructors to see within days - sometimes hours - whether students are struggling with a concept. Employers using simulations can measure training outcomes instantly. Workforce boards, like those in Texas and Colorado, are now detecting emerging skills shortages through real-time credential verification data, not retroactive surveys.

Colorado's workforce pilots show how near-real-time feedback can redirect learners into renewable energy programs before shortages intensify. Texas' Tri-Agency Initiative has compressed the cycle of curriculum alignment to respond within months, rather than years, to labor shifts. In New York, SUNY's analytics platforms provide faculty and policymakers with almost immediate indicators of student persistence and success. Tennessee's own predictive advising tools, linked to THEC and TBR data, are beginning to achieve similar results - spotting at-risk learners mid-semester and intervening before failure becomes final.

Yet perpetual loops demand caution. Without careful design, systems can confuse velocity with validity. WHO reminds us in its digital health frameworks that "more frequent feedback" does not always equal "better feedback," especially if data is biased or overwhelming. Gartner warns that organizations that chase every new signal risk "dashboard fatigue." Thus, our task is to refine not only speed but discernment: identifying which signals matter, when action should occur, and how to balance immediacy with wisdom.

Tennessee's lesson is that compressed loops succeed when tied to trust. Faculty need confidence that dashboards reflect context, not just numbers. Employers need assurance that credential signals correspond to real competence. Policymakers need transparency to act with legitimacy. Without trust, perpetual loops risk collapsing into perpetual doubt.

The OODA Framework for Learning Systems

At the individual level, OODA empowers learners to self-regulate. They observe their own performance through credential wallets or class dashboards, orient to gaps, decide on corrective steps, and act - sometimes within a single learning session. A working student at Motlow State, for example, might see an alert about math readiness, access adaptive OER, and close a skill gap before the next assessment. This autonomy transforms learners from passive recipients of evaluation to active agents of their own progression.

At the institutional level, OODA gives colleges and training providers an adaptive spine. Tennessee community colleges, for example, aggregate student performance data to identify program-level gaps. Instead of waiting years for program review cycles, they can intervene within terms. Colorado's exchange pilots demonstrate this at scale - institutions adjust course content based on patterns observed across multiple campuses. SUNY has embedded OODA logic into its microcredential rollouts, ensuring curricula are not static but continuously aligned with labor market shifts.

At the ecosystem level, OODA informs entire regions. Tennessee's Department of Labor, working with THEC and TBR, uses labor signals to reallocate resources toward advanced manufacturing and cybersecurity. Texas' tri-agency framework orients entire education systems to labor trends. Colorado's renewable energy pathways and SUNY's healthcare pipelines show similar alignment. At this scale, OODA is not about one learner or institution but about keeping entire talent ecosystems resilient.

When individual, institutional, and ecosystem loops align, systems become self-correcting. Brookings calls this "learning ecosystems," where adaptive feedback keeps entire regions competitive. The EU's Digital Decade framework makes similar arguments for sovereign but interoperable feedback systems. The risk is fragmentation if loops are isolated. The opportunity is resilience when loops are synchronized.

Data as a Public Utility

OODA-driven feedback requires data that is timely, accessible, and trustworthy. Data must be treated not as proprietary commodity but as a public utility. Open standards ensure that credentials and performance data can be shared across platforms without costly translation. Privacy-by-design keeps learners in control of what data travels, when, and with whom. Mutual benefit agreements ensure that no single party
- employer, university, or government - extracts disproportionate value from shared data.

Colorado has pioneered open credential registries that employers and institutions can both access. Texas has created state-level data compacts to share student outcomes across agencies. New York's SUNY OER and skills frameworks emphasize data portability across institutions. Tennessee's UIS pilots echo these moves by embedding blockchain-based verification that learners can carry with them. UNESCO insists that portability must respect cultural and legal contexts, while WHO reminds us that equity must travel with data to prevent exclusion.

The EU's AI Act requires that accountability metadata move with algorithms, a lesson applicable to credentials and learning data. NIST frames interoperability as essential to risk mitigation. Brookings argues that public confidence in education and workforce systems depends on open, auditable standards. Tennessee can lead nationally by advancing data as a civic trust rather than a corporate asset.

The utility metaphor is deliberate: just as electricity and clean water are prerequisites for modern life, trusted, portable data is the infrastructure of a feedback society. Without it, OODA cannot scale beyond local pilots. With it, feedback can become a shared civic good.

Closing the Loop Faster

In old models, a mismatch between curriculum and market demand might take years to identify and correct. In Tennessee, for example, misalignment in nursing supply often persisted across legislative cycles. In a feedback society, employers can now flag shortages immediately through hiring data. UIS-integrated learning platforms can adapt curricula within weeks. Adaptive OER modules can be deployed in real time to address gaps.

Colorado's renewable energy programs adjust rapidly to employer demand signals. Texas has reduced time-to-curriculum-change by embedding employer data into education dashboards. New York's SUNY programs integrate industry microcredentials mid-term. Tennessee's TBR pilots with labor-linked dashboards shorten the distance between market signal and curricular response.

McKinsey estimates that shortening loop times could reduce workforce mismatches by up to 20% globally, with measurable productivity gains. Gartner emphasizes that organizations that compress loops outperform peers in agility. Yet speed introduces risks: unverified signals may cause over-correction; poorly timed interventions can create instability. WHO warns against "chasing noise" in health AI, a lesson equally relevant to education.

The challenge is to combine velocity with validation. Tennessee's experience suggests that loops must be both fast and thoughtful. The art is not speed for speed's sake but speed in service of equity, relevance, and resilience.

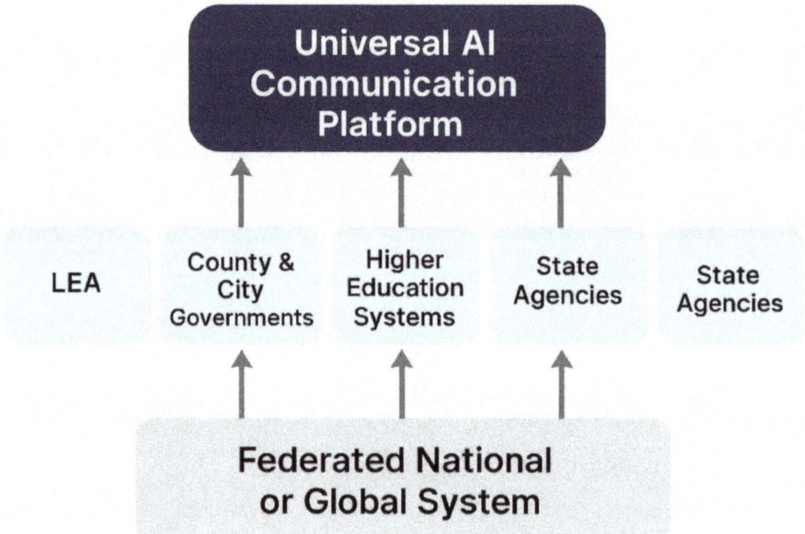

References - Chapter 8

1. Tennessee Board of Regents (TBR). Fast Facts and System Reports 2024-2025. tbr.edu

2. Tennessee Higher Education Commission (THEC). Tennessee Higher Education Fact Book 2024-2025. tn.gov/thec

3. Tennessee Department of Labor & Workforce Development. Occupational Projections and Labor Market Information. tn.gov/workforce

4. Colorado Department of Higher Education. Credential Quality Framework; Colorado Education Exchange Pilot.highered. colorado.gov

5. Texas Higher Education Coordinating Board / Tri-Agency Workforce Initiative. Building a Talent Strong Texas.highered. texas.gov

6. State University of New York (SUNY). Microcredentials and OER Services. suny.edu

7. National Institute of Standards and Technology (NIST). AI Risk Management Framework; Cybersecurity Guidance for Education and Workforce Systems. nist.gov

8. U.S. Department of Education, Office of Educational Technology. Advancing Digital Equity and AI in Learning. ed.gov

9. European Commission. Artificial Intelligence Act; European Digital Identity Wallet; Quantum Flagship; Digital Decade Strategy. europa.eu; ec.europa.eu

10. World Health Organization (WHO). Ethics and Governance of Artificial Intelligence for Health; Equity in Digital Health Systems. who.int

11. UNESCO. Recommendation on the Ethics of AI; Guidelines on OER and Equity in Digital Learning. unesco.org

12. McKinsey & Company. The State of AI in 2024; Future of Work: Skills, Talent, and Continuous Learning. mckinsey.com

13. Brookings Institution. AI Governance and Equity; Continuous Learning and Workforce Policy; Trust in Digital Economies. brookings.edu

14. Gartner. Trust-by-Design in AI; Real-Time Feedback Loops; Interoperability & Immersive Learning Trends. gartner.com

15. Boyd, John. The Essence of Winning and Losing: OODA Loop Lectures. Defense Analysis Archive.

16. OECD. AI in Education: Policy for Continuous Learning and Trust. oecd.org

Chapter 9 - Designing Trust Networks: Governance for the AI Age

If the feedback society is our nervous system, trust networks are our immune system. They decide what gets in, what stays out, and how the system recovers when compromised. In an AI-driven age, trust shifts from interpersonal confidence to systemic assurance. Identity, skill, and intent must be verified instantly, across borders, without compromising privacy or agency. For Tennessee, and for states like Colorado, Texas, and New York, building trust networks is not just a technical task - it is a civic imperative.

Why Trust is the New Infrastructure …

Without trust, UIS is a database, OER is a file repository, and credentials are decorative. With trust, identity is authenticated, credentials are verified, and records carry provenance. The EU's AI Act and Digital Identity frameworks demonstrate what infrastructure-grade trust looks like. NIST's AI Risk Management Framework emphasizes accountability, explainability, and auditability as non-negotiables.

Brookings frames trust as the "currency" of digital economies; McKinsey shows the productivity unlocked when verification is instant. Tennessee employers already report faster hiring when credentials are verifiable. Colorado's credential exchanges reduce friction. Texas' tri-agency systems create trust in statewide recognition. SUNY's microcredentials gain credibility through transparent frameworks. Trust, in this sense, is infrastructure that makes the rest of the system usable.

The risk is fragility: a single breach can undermine confidence across networks. The opportunity is scale: once trust is embedded, mobility and collaboration accelerate. Trust is no longer an enabler; it is the backbone.

Principles of Trust Network Design

Designing trust networks requires balance between security, transparency, and agency. Distributed verification ensures no single entity monopolizes authority.

Privacy by default keeps individuals in control of their records. Transparency of process allows audits of algorithms and standards. Adaptability to context acknowledges that "trust" is culturally and legally defined differently across jurisdictions.

Colorado's exchange uses distributed verification among institutions and employers. Texas' frameworks embed privacy safeguards. SUNY's OER platforms practice transparency by making processes public. Tennessee's blockchain pilots show adaptability by including contextual data. UNESCO, WHO, and NIST all stress that human dignity must remain central.

A trust network cannot be an opaque black box. It must be a civic framework where participants understand how verification occurs, and where accountability is visible. This transparency builds legitimacy and prevents trust from becoming another vector for exclusion.

The Role of Blockchain and Beyond

Blockchain offers immutable records, decentralized control, and time-stamped provenance. Tennessee's Metaversity pilots, Colorado's credential exchange, and SUNY's experiments all leverage blockchain for verification. Yet blockchain is insufficient alone. Trust networks also require AI-enabled anomaly detection, quantum-resilient encryption, and federated identity systems.

The EU's Quantum Flagship anticipates the need for quantum-resistant trust architectures. NIST and OECD have begun mapping pathways for cryptographic transition. Gartner argues that hybrid trust stacks - blockchain plus AI plus encryption
- are the realistic future.

Blockchain contributes permanence, but trust requires adaptability. The challenge is designing plural systems that reinforce one another rather than rely on a single tool.

Trust at Human Speed

Trust must match the speed of decision-making. A hiring manager in Tokyo should verify a Tennessee credential instantly. A Lagos licensing authority should confirm a Toronto nursing certificate before the candidate arrives. A São Paulo admissions officer should validate a Kenyan transcript without weeks of delay.

Colorado's systems already allow multi-institutional verification in minutes. Texas' statewide frameworks create uniformity across regions. SUNY's integration with employer systems shortens verification cycles. The EU's interoperability work shows cross-border feasibility.

The risk is lag: if trust verification lags behind decision-making, opportunity is lost. The opportunity is velocity: instant verification enables collaboration, hiring, and learning at scale.

Governing the Trust Network

Trust networks are technical but also political, economic, and cultural. Politically, they must respect sovereignty. Economically, they must be affordable for small institutions. Culturally, they must reflect diverse norms of evidence. Governance must be multi-stakeholder, with rotating leadership and transparent rules.

Tennessee's workforce councils, Colorado's governance committees, Texas' tri-agency boards, and SUNY's public processes demonstrate inclusive governance. UNESCO calls for marginalized voices at the table; WHO warns that exclusion perpetuates inequity. Brookings argues for legitimacy through openness.

Governance is the difference between a trust network that empowers and one that entrenches power. It must be designed as a commons, not a cartel.

Trust Erosion and Recovery

Breach is inevitable. A fraudulent issuer or compromised registry can undermine confidence. Recovery requires rapid incident response, redundancy, and public accountability. Continuous audits prevent small cracks from becoming failures. Shared incident databases spread lessons across jurisdictions.

The EU's conformity assessments, NIST's continuous monitoring, and Gartner's resilience models all support proactive recovery planning. Tennessee's risk frameworks, Colorado's audits, Texas' redundancy plans, and SUNY's transparency requirements provide state-level examples.

The lesson is humility: trust is fragile. Designing for failure and recovery is part of stewardship.

The Interdependence of Trust and Equity

Trust networks without equity amplify inequality. Marginalized learners may lack access to verification. Small institutions may be priced out. Non-dominant languages may be ignored. Equity must be structural: multilingual services, tiered pricing or subsidies, inclusion of local validators.

UNESCO frames this as cultural dignity. WHO insists equity must anchor health AI. Brookings stresses legitimacy. Tennessee's rural learners, Colorado's frontier communities, Texas' urban diversity, and SUNY's global student base all prove the point: equity builds resilience.

The risk is exclusion; the opportunity is legitimacy. Trust must be universal to be durable.

From Trust Networks to Trust Economies-and the Trust Dividend

When trust networks function, they enable trust economies. Cross-border talent exchanges bypass redundancy. Shared R&D pipelines link universities and industries. Real-time workforce deployment supports crisis response. The friction of proving capability falls away, and collaboration accelerates.

McKinsey quantifies the productivity dividend. Brookings shows how trust builds civic confidence. Gartner tracks cost savings. Tennessee's pilots, Colorado's exchanges, Texas' systems, and SUNY's networks all validate the theory.

The dividend is not only economic. It is cultural capital - the belief that systems can be both fair and secure, both global and local. That belief is the precondition for innovation, resilience, and shared progress.

References - Chapters 9

1. Tennessee Board of Regents (TBR). Fast Facts and System Reports 2024-2025. tbr.edu

2. Tennessee Higher Education Commission (THEC). Tennessee Higher Education Fact Book 2024-2025. tn.gov/thec

3. Tennessee Department of Labor & Workforce Development. Occupational Projections and Labor Market Information. tn.gov/workforce

4. Colorado Department of Higher Education. Credential Quality Framework; Colorado Education Exchange Pilot.highered. colorado.gov

5. Texas Higher Education Coordinating Board / Tri-Agency Workforce Initiative. Building a Talent Strong Texas.highered. texas.gov

6. State University of New York (SUNY). Microcredentials and OER Services. suny.edu

7. National Institute of Standards and Technology (NIST). AI Risk Management Framework; Cybersecurity Guidance for Education and Workforce Systems. nist.gov

8. U.S. Department of Education, Office of Educational Technology. Advancing Digital Equity and AI in Learning. ed.gov

9. European Commission. Artificial Intelligence Act; European Digital Identity Wallet; Quantum Flagship; Digital Decade Strategy. europa.eu

10. European Commission. Artificial Intelligence Act; European Digital Identity Wallet; Quantum Flagship; Digital Decade Strategy. ec.europa.eu

11. World Health Organization (WHO). Ethics and Governance of Artificial Intelligence for Health; Equity in Digital Health Systems. who.int

12. UNESCO. Recommendation on the Ethics of AI; Guidelines on OER and Equity in Digital Learning. unesco.org

13. McKinsey & Company. The State of AI in 2024; Future of Work: Skills, Talent, and Continuous Learning. mckinsey.com

14. Brookings Institution. AI Governance and Equity; Continuous Learning and Workforce Policy; Trust in Digital Economies. brookings.edu

15. Gartner. Trust-by-Design in AI; Real-Time Feedback Loops; Interoperability & Immersive Learning Trends. gartner.com

16. Boyd, John. The Essence of Winning and Losing: OODA Loop Lectures. Defense Analysis Archive.

17. OECD. AI in Education: Policy for Continuous Learning and Trust. oecd.org

Chapter 10 - The Creative and the Builder: AI at the Intersection of Imagination and Implementation

We have established the scaffolding - governance frameworks (Chapter 4), Universally Integrated Systems (Chapter 5), credentialing architectures (Chapter 6), adaptive learning ecosystems (Chapter 7), real-time feedback societies (Chapter 8), and trust networks (Chapter 9). These are not abstract constructs; they are the working infrastructure of the AI age. Yet infrastructure, by itself, does not move a community. People do. The decisive variable of the next decade will be the human archetypes who can imagine, translate, validate, and normalize AI-enabled systems - not as a parade of hype, but as a disciplined choreography of learning, work, and civic trust. In that choreography, I locate four roles whose interplay determines whether AI becomes a force for flourishing or fragmentation: Creatives, Builders, Laggers, and Followers.

The practical question, then, is not simply what we should build, but who will build it, how they will co-design with artificial, augmented, and awareness intelligence, and which trust qualities will keep the system legitimate as it scales. This chapter argues that the center of gravity is a triad of trust - transparency, translucence, and transmutability - applied consistently across archetypes and contexts. It is how we keep systems open enough to invite participation, protected enough to remain secure, and flexible enough to evolve with context. Tennessee's work in credential verification, Colorado's exchange pilots, Texas's tri-agency alignments, and SUNY's microcredentialing stance all point to this conclusion: human roles make the difference between machinery and mission.

We believe it is important to discuss the three forms of intelligence in play. First, Artificial Intelligence (AI): machine-driven systems that learn, reason, and act, increasingly autonomously in narrow domains. AI is no longer a laboratory curiosity; it is the backbone of adaptive OER, the matching engine inside credential wallets, and the recommendation layer in workforce dashboards. In Tennessee, AI helps align TBR curricula to labor signals from the Department of Labor; in New York, SUNY's programs embed AI to personalize pathways; in Texas, tri-agency analytics use AI to reduce time-to-alignment; and in Colorado, predictive tools steer learners into renewable energy roles before shortages harden. Yet NIST is clear: AI must be trustworthy by design - explainable, reliable, secure - and WHO reminds us that without equity guardrails, AI can magnify disparities rather than reduce them. AI's promise, then, is power; its peril is opacity.

Second, Augmented Intelligence (AuI): human-machine partnerships designed to extend human capacity, not replace it. AuI is the educator's co-pilot, the nurse's decision support, the advisor's early-warning signal. It does not replace judgment; it sharpens it. Tennessee's advising pilots illustrate this well: faculty remain in command while AuI surfaces timely, contextualized signals. In Colorado's exchange, AuI helps registrars reconcile records across institutions. In Texas, AuI compresses curriculum refresh cycles; in New York, AuI pairs microcredentials to employer projects. UNESCO's ethic is unambiguous here: augmentation must enhance dignity and expand agency, or it will be resisted and rightly so. AuI succeeds when people feel more capable - not more controlled.

Third, Awareness Intelligence (AwI): the capacity - human and, one day, AI-augmented - for meta-cognition: understanding not just how to act, but why, and toward what end. AwI is ethics with memory, context with foresight, governance with humility. It asks whether a perfectly optimized model is socially legitimate, culturally consonant, or democratically accountable. Brookings calls this the "legibility of intent"; UNESCO frames it as the right to shape technology's moral itinerary; WHO places AwI at the heart of equity. AwI is the difference between deploying a predictive model and deciding whether that deployment serves human flourishing, especially for communities historically left at the margins.

Across all three, a trust triad mediates behavior: transparency, translucence, and transmutability. Transparency makes decisions and data flows visible enough to evaluate. Translucence balances openness with privacy and security - showing enough to earn trust while protecting the sensitive. Transmutability ensures the system can adapt - to new standards, new risks, new cultures - without breaking. The EU's AI Act operationalizes this logic in law; NIST operationalizes it in method; Gartner recasts it as "trust-by-design." This triad is not rhetorical; it is the steering geometry for complex, human-in-the-loop systems.

Additionally, we have the four human archetypes in AI-Enabled futures. The Creatives who are the vision catalysts - the people who see possibility before the lines are painted. They translate weak signals into durable concepts, cross disciplines by instinct, and hold space for ambiguity when others rush to closure. In our Tennessee work, Creatives were the first to imagine a learner-controlled wallet, a microcredential that speaks both global and local, and a UIS that moves as easily between counties as across borders. In New York, Creatives inside SUNY reframed OER from "free content" into an adaptive commons; in Colorado, they reimagined renewable energy pathways; in Texas, they envisioned statewide alignment as a living system rather than a compliance burden.

Their risk is detachment from feasibility. Without Builders, policy, and budget gravity, even brilliant ideas can float free of implementation. Here the trust triad disciplines imagination: transparency clarifies objectives and constraints; translucence protects early-stage IP and community-sensitive ideas from premature scrutiny; transmutability gives permission to pivot when data, context, or equity demands it. Brookings reminds us that legitimacy attaches to ideas when their assumptions are inspectable and their social impacts are considered. The Creative's craft, therefore, is not just invention; it is responsible imagination.

Creatives thrive in co-design studios where AuI scaffolds brainstorming with evidence: model cards that surface risks, equity impact notes that travel with concepts, and scenario simulators that test ideas across cultures and jurisdictions. With AwI in the room, Creatives interrogate ends, not only means: Who benefits? Who bears risk? What does "good" look like in ten years? When anchored by the triad, their prototypes become pathways others are willing to walk.

The measure of the Creative is not the novelty of the idea, but its trajectory into practice. In a trusted ecosystem, that trajectory is visible, critique is welcomed, and iteration is celebrated. Vision, then, becomes a public good - not a private performance.

The Builders are the translators of vision into working systems. They absorb ambiguity and produce scaffolds: data schemas, APIs, model governance, cybersecurity controls, audit trails, and user experiences that actually work on Tuesday morning. In Tennessee, Builders turned blockchain rhetoric into verified credentials that a hiring manager could trust. In Colorado, they stitched registries into usable exchanges; in Texas, they operationalized tri-agency data contracts; in New York, they integrated microcredentials with employer verification and OER pipelines.

Their risk is over-fitting to process: mistaking standards for outcomes, compliance for legitimacy, or scalability for value. The trust triad keeps them elastic. Transparency in development cycles (roadmaps, change logs, test plans) builds user and stakeholder confidence. Translucence in architecture hides the right things - keys, attack surfaces, proprietary methods - to preserve security and defensibility. Transmutability is the anti-rigidity clause: modular components, versioned taxonomies, and policy "escape hatches" that allow fast compliance with new rules (EU AI Act), new risk guidance (NIST AI RMF), or new cultural requirements (UNESCO's inclusion principles).

Builders excel when AuI becomes their quality co-pilot - suggesting test coverage, flagging bias regressions, rendering explainer views, and checking conformance requirements automatically. With AwI present, Builders ask governance questions in the design meeting, not after launch: Who can appeal a model decision? Where is human override? How is harm reported and repaired? Their deliverable is not only software or policy; it is operational trust.

The hallmark of a mature Builder culture is "change without collapse." Systems can be reconfigured without breaking the social contract. That is not an accident; it is the outcome of designing for transmutability from day one.

The Laggers are the late adopters - the teams and institutions that move when systems are proven and stable. They are often caricatured as obstacles to progress; I see them as guardians of reliability and memory. They validate systems in diverse, real-world contexts, catch edge cases enthusiasts overlook, and prevent us from burning trust on the altar of speed. In Tennessee, Laggers insisted we show longitudinal value before scaling wallet pilots statewide. In Colorado and Texas, they pressed for stress tests and failure drills. In SUNY, they demanded that microcredentials demonstrate employer recognition before entering program catalogs.

Their risk is missing the window - delaying transformation until the cost of inaction is higher than the risk of change. The trust triad invites them in without forcing a leap of faith. Transparency in performance data, incident reports, and cost-benefit evidence builds adoption readiness. Translucence offers early previews - sandboxes, limited pilots, safe-to-fail zones - without overexposure to complexity. Transmutability reassures them that systems can adjust to proven needs and local contexts over time.

Laggers become allies when AuI lowers the cognitive burden of adoption: guided workflows, explainer overlays, and risk dashboards that speak their language. With AwI engaged, their lived constraints are dignified, not dismissed: staffing cycles, accreditation timelines, rural broadband, union rules. In my experience, when we design with Laggers rather than around them, we gain hard-won legitimacy.

A healthy ecosystem turns Laggers into late validators who, once convinced, become powerful champions of scale. That pivot is the quiet engine of durable reform.

The Followers are the end-users who normalize systems at scale - students, patients, job seekers, citizens, fans. They supply the usage patterns, edge cases, and feedback that reveal whether we built tools or toys. In Tennessee, Followers made or broke our pilots: if the wallet didn't reduce friction, if adaptive OER didn't actually help, if verification didn't speed hiring, the project stalled. In New York, Colorado, and Texas, the pattern holds: mass adoption follows evident benefit.

Their risk is vulnerability - to dark patterns, exploitative data practices, or opaque algorithms. The trust triad is their bill of rights. Transparency in user rights, model use, and data practices sustains engagement. Translucence in decision logic - layered explanations, not math lectures - fosters understanding without overload.

Transmutability ensures interfaces and policies adapt to lived experience: accessibility needs, language, bandwidth, and device constraints.

Followers become co-designers when AuI turns feedback into feature direction (not just telemetry), and when AwI anchors choices in dignity: defaults that protect, consent that is meaningful, recourse that is real. The metric here is simple: Do people feel more capable, informed, and respected after contact with the system?

When the answer is "yes," followers transform into a civic asset - the largest, most diverse quality assurance team a society could hope to inherit.

Our archetypes and governance deserve a dynamic matrix. Governance must weave the triad into how it engages each archetype. With Creatives, governance creates horizon-scanning and safe-to-experiment spaces that surface both possibility and risk, tying imagination to measurable social goals. With Builders, it invests in assurance factories - shared test suites, model cards, audit templates, and red-team exercises - so operational integrity is not an afterthought. With Laggers, it formalizes evidence gates - adoption triggers based on safety, reliability, and cost data. With Followers, it mandates rights notices, appeal channels, and clarity of consent in language people actually use.

The matrix should cycle influence, not concentrate it. Early in innovation, Creatives and Builders have more weight; as solutions mature, Laggers and

Followers rebalance direction with proof and experience. Brookings calls this the "diplomacy of governance" - a structured tension that prevents any single actor from dictating outcomes. NIST provides the scaffolding; the EU's AI Act provides a floor; UNESCO and WHO ensure equity and dignity remain non-negotiable.

In practice, this looks like multistakeholder councils with rotating leadership and transparent rulemaking. Tennessee's cross-sector tables, Colorado's exchange governance, Texas's tri-agency councils, and SUNY's public processes are working models. The virtue is not speed alone; it is legitimacy with momentum.

A dynamic matrix does one more thing: it remembers. Incident registries, change logs, and post-mortems travel with systems so tomorrow's decisions benefit from yesterday's lessons.

There is an obvious need to co-design across intelligence types. For example, AI + Creative: Transparent ideation spaces balanced with translucent IP protections let teams imagine boldly while shielding the sensitive during incubation. AuI can synthesize literature, surface analogies across fields, and generate early prototypes; AwI interrogates purposes and potential harms. In Tennessee's Metaversity work, this pairing turned sketches into testable pilots without burning trust.

AI + Builder: Transparent performance metrics and compliance evidence, paired with transmutable pipelines, keep shipping safe and fast. AuI flags regressions and regulatory drift; AwI keeps the human in command by embedding override points, appeal routes, and harm reporting. Colorado's and SUNY's systems demonstrate that when Builders co-design with AI, reliability and explainability rise together.

AI + Lagger: Translucent previews - sandboxes, shadow runs, and pilot dashboards - de-risk adoption without demanding faith. Transparency in risk profiles and costs turns caution into prudence. Transmutability ensures local constraints can be honored during rollout. Texas's phased adoption playbooks show how to move late adopters with respect, not pressure.

AI + Follower: Clear use policies, layered explanations, and transmutable interfaces that adapt to ability, language, and device create dignity at the edge. AuI personalizes support; AwI ensures defaults favor the user. In all four pairings, the triad is the choreography; co-design is the practice; humanism is the anchor.

When we design these pairings intentionally, the result is not "human vs. machine" but humanism with machinery - systems that learn us even as we learn them. This alignment or sorts allows us to pair and share while propelling society through learning adaptable trust.

Adaptable trust is the operating advantage of the next decade. Leaders build legitimacy by practicing transparency that informs, translucence that protects, and transmutability that welcomes change. Partners - across universities, employers, agencies, and communities - co-design systems that anticipate both innovation and regulation. Laggers are brought forward with visible proof and adaptive safeguards. Followers are supported with clear rights, visible benefits, and evolving features that reflect lived realities.

In Tennessee, adaptable trust is the difference between a pilot and a policy. In Colorado and Texas, it is how multi-institution systems survive leadership changes. In New York, it keeps OER and microcredentials credible with employers and students. McKinsey quantifies the productivity gains of trust; Brookings explains its civic dividend; Gartner traces its operational payback; the EU, NIST, UNESCO, and WHO codify its principles in law and guidance.

Adaptable trust is not soft. It is hard infrastructure for change. It gives us permission to move fast and fix things - to adjust without apology when evidence demands it. It makes the continuous improvement of Chapter 8 and the governance realism of Chapter 4 feel like one system, not competing agendas.

If we get this right, trust ceases to be a cost center and becomes the flywheel of adoption, and in turn this calls for co-designing. Perhaps this is a zone of approximal development too.

The AI age will not be led by one archetype, one sector, or one form of intelligence. It will be propelled by co-designed systems where Creatives imagine, Builders implement, Laggers stabilize, and Followers scale. The triad keeps each contribution aligned: transparency builds clarity, translucence builds confidence, and transmutability builds resilience. Tennessee, Colorado, Texas, and New York have already proven that when we convene these roles around shared evidence and shared purpose, innovation becomes stewardship.

This is not a call for harmony without friction. It is a call for productive tension -

the kind that sharpens ideas, strengthens systems, and dignifies people. It asks us to center Awareness Intelligence so our means never outrun our ends. It asks us to practice augmentation as empowerment, not control. And it asks us to govern for the long arc: building institutions that can learn, adapt, and include.

The horizon of this work is clear. If we steward AI with humanism - anchored in equity, accountable to evidence, and open to iteration - we will convert potential into prosperity with dignity. If we do not, the same technologies will exacerbate divides we already struggle to cross. The choice is not technical; it is moral. The work is not someday; it is now.

So we design - together - and we keep the loop human.

References - Chapter 10

1. Tennessee Board of Regents (TBR). Fast Facts and System Reports 2024-2025. tbr.edu

2. Tennessee Higher Education Commission (THEC). Tennessee Higher Education Fact Book 2024-2025. tn.gov/thec

3. Tennessee Department of Labor & Workforce Development. Occupational Projections and Labor Market Information. tn.gov/workforce

4. Colorado Department of Higher Education. Credential Quality Framework; Colorado Education Exchange Pilot. highered.colorado.gov

5. Texas Higher Education Coordinating Board / Tri-Agency Workforce Initiative. Building a Talent Strong Texas; Workforce Alignment Reports. highered.texas.gov

6. State University of New York (SUNY). Microcredentials and OER Services. suny.edu

7. National Institute of Standards and Technology (NIST). AI Risk Management Framework; Trustworthy & Responsible AI guidance. nist.gov

8. U.S. Department of Education, Office of Educational Technology. Advancing Digital Equity and AI in Learning. ed.gov

9. European Commission. Artificial Intelligence Act; European Digital Identity Wallet; Digital Decade Strategy; Quantum Flagship. europa.eu; ec.europa.eu

10. UNESCO. Recommendation on the Ethics of AI; OER and inclusion guidance. unesco.org/unesdoc.unesco.org

11. World Health Organization (WHO). Ethics and Governance of

Artificial Intelligence for Health; Equity in Digital Health Systems. who.int McKinsey & Company. State of AI 2024; Future of Work and Skills. mckinsey.com

12. Brookings Institution. Global AI Governance; Skills & Workforce; Legitimacy and Standards. brookings.edu

13. Gartner. Trust-by-Design; AI Governance; Interoperability & Adoption Playbooks. gartner.com

Chapter 11 - Games, Sports, and the Analytics of Performance: Paradigm Shifts

If you want to see how humans and machines will truly co-design the future, do not start in a boardroom-start courtside, pitch-side, track-side. Sports compress experimentation, feedback, iteration, and consequence into the span of a quarter or a heat. The arena is a living lab where pressure and passion meet telemetry and tape, where a single possession can surface signal from noise. In that crucible, the blend of artificial intelligence (AI), augmented intelligence (AuI), and awareness intelligence (AwI) becomes visible, testable, and-most importantly-teachable.

Because sport is not merely technical; it is human. It is story and rivalry, muscle memory and meaning, an ever-renewing relationship between what we can measure and what we must feel. That makes it the perfect domain for exercising the trust triad as an invisible referee: transparency that clarifies, translucence that protects, and transmutability that adapts.

The stadium therefore becomes a microcosm of societal systems we are building elsewhere in this work: Universally Integrated Systems (UIS) for credentialing, adaptive OER for learning, trust networks for verification. In sports, these abstractions take on sweat and stakes. You can see a dashboard's recommendation influence a substitution pattern, then watch it succeed or fail in front of thousands.
You can trace how data provenance and equipment standards convert into confidence for coaches, players, and fans. The clarity and consequence sharpen governance questions that sometimes go fuzzy in slower-moving institutions.

Our Tennessee lens reinforces this pragmatism. The same instinct that makes a coach ask, "Show me the film," should govern AI in the classroom or on the shop floor: reveal method, reveal context, reveal evidence of improvement-not to worship data, but to discipline it. Colorado, Texas, and New York offer parallel lessons: statewide high school and collegiate programs trialing sensor-based training, athletic departments adopting video-AI breakdowns, and conference offices codifying how augmented tech may be used in competitive windows. The point is not novelty. The point is responsible advantage-performance that honors the person.

In this chapter, I will map two intertwined arcs. First, the technology arc-from analytics to haptics-showing how we move from descriptive to prescriptive to embodied intelligence. Second, the human arc-how our archetypes (Creatives, Builders, Laggers, Followers, Collectors too) dance with the trust triad to keep sport both advanced and authentic. The payoff is not only better play; it is a portable template for co-design in education, workforce, and civic life.

The analytics era in sports is deep into predictive and optimal analytics. Sports analytics has traveled far beyond box scores. Player-tracking beacons translate motion into geometry; computer vision turns frames into features; models infer the invisible-fatigue curve, injury risk, lineup synergy, even clutch probability under crowd pressure. The best systems do not replace judgment; they make judgment more precise. A coach reads a rotation chart with context-matchups, foul trouble, an athlete's emotional state-and then decides. The algorithm's job is to offer a clean window, not to lock the door. That is AuI at work: human-centered, human-paced, human-accountable.

Yet analytics is not purely additive. It reshapes practice. When AI surfaces a biomechanical inefficiency, the film room expands into the weight room and the training table. Rep schemes change; rest protocols adapt; travel schedules flex. Fans feel it too. Broadcast overlays explain expected points added, pitch tunneling, or off-ball gravity in ways that deepen-not cheapen-the spectacle. Transparency here builds legitimacy: when stakeholders can see how insight is derived and how it is bounded, they accept that "smart" is still governed by "fair."

The limits are as instructive as the breakthroughs. Data has blind spots: a sensor cannot see a family crisis, a camera cannot capture courage. Without AwI-our meta-cognitive ethic-we risk elevating precise nonsense. That is why governance must require model cards and usage charters in sport as in school: what the model is (and is not) designed to do, what data it used (and did not), what error bars mean (and do not). Translucence matters too. We can reveal the what and why without exposing a player's sensitive medical record or a team's protected playbook.

Transmutability completes the triad: when the league updates a rule or the science updates a standard, the analytic pipeline must adapt without tearing the fabric of competition.

States are already practicing these balances. Colorado's collegiate programs have piloted sensor-informed training with written guardrails; Texas high school associations have defined windows when tech is allowed; New York's SUNY athletics has paired analytics literacy with athlete consent education.

Tennessee can anchor this with a simple principle transferable to every domain we've discussed: show your work, protect the person, and keep the system change-ready.

The haptic revolution has started to move from skips to bounds. We are entering the era where analytics jumps off the screen and onto the body. Haptics is no longer a buzz in your pocket; it is full-spectrum tactile coaching. Imagine compression sleeves modulating micro-vibration to cue shooting form mid-flight, smart shin guards nudging foot angle on first touch, bat grips signaling minute timing adjustments against a specific pitch profile. Helmets can deliver subtle alerts for blindside pressure-informative, not startling-while maintaining strict safety thresholds. Track spikes can cue stride length and ground contact in real time; even bowling wrist wraps can stabilize release consistency via micro-haptics. Yes, even corn hole on the back porch becomes a testing ground for adoption curves-because if your uncle can learn to love a nudge toward proper arc, your front-line workforce can too.

Haptics changes pedagogy. We have taught primarily with eyes and ears; now touch becomes a learning channel. This democratizes coaching: a JV athlete in rural Tennessee gains access to embodied guidance once reserved for elite camps. It also raises new equity questions: who pays, who trains, who maintains, who audits for safety and fairness? Governance must lean into all three intelligences: AI to interpret and prescribe, AuI to present and pace, AwI to decide where we must stop. Transparency translates to visible standards and safety certifications; translucence to protecting proprietary algorithms from copycat exploitation while still proving fairness; transmutability to OTA firmware updates that keep devices aligned with evolving rules and science.

The athlete's body is sacred space; the fan's experience is communal ritual. Haptics must respect both. Consent must be informed, revocable, and logged. Data minimization should be non-negotiable. Competitive integrity demands league-level conformance tests and random audits. And cultural fit matters: what a basketball crowd celebrates in New York might feel foreign in a Tennessee gym-local norms must inform rollout. "Glocal" deployment (global standards, local practice) keeps the experience human.

Most importantly, we must keep the human at the center of the feedback loop. Haptics is the whisper; the athlete is the one who chooses. When the nudge becomes a shove, we have lost the plot. When the nudge becomes a shared language between player and coach, we have something worth scaling.

It is not clear how to define the Archetypes in the sports ecosystem.

However, in sport, the Creatives redesign possibility. They sketch new sets, spawn novel defensive looks, envision fan engagement modes that stitch onsite and online into one experience. Their best ally is AuI-simulation boards that preview how a formation behaves against archetypal opponents, narrative tools that translate complexity into coaching language, and risk explorers that flag where an innovation could backfire. The trust triad tempers exuberance: transparent objectives to judge success, translucent cover to incubate ideas, and transmutable playbooks that can pivot mid-season if a rule or meta-game shifts.

The Builders turn imagination into kit and code: the haptic sleeve, the computer-vision pipeline, the scouting database, the stadium's mixed-reality stack. Their craft lives in standards, safety, and scale. Transparency looks like published device safety metrics and independent certifications; translucence protects kernels and keys; transmutability is design for change-modular hardware, versioned APIs, and fallbacks for degraded conditions. Builders make trust tangible: when the gear is certified, the feed is reliable, and the updates are quiet and frequent, adoption feels like common sense.

The Laggers-the coach who needs proof, the league that waits for multi-season data, the player who wants to see a teammate benefit first-serve an essential function: they keep us honest. We court them with longitudinal injury-reduction studies, transparent performance evidence, and safe-to-try pilots (pre-season, scrimmage windows, limited competitions). Translucence avoids overwhelming them; transmutability offers incremental pathways rather than all-or-nothing leaps. When Laggers finally move, they stabilize the innovation-not as hype, but as habit.

The Followers normalize everything. Youth leagues, weekend athletes, and fans decide what becomes culture. They need clear disclosures on data use, layered explanations for odds or insights, and interfaces that adapt to preference and comfort-basic stats for some, full AR overlays for others. When Followers feel respected, they give the system patience and feedback. When they feel extracted, they revolt. Respect is a design choice; so is revolt.

Sports are a Global Trust Network. Sport already operates as a transnational trust web: governing bodies certify rules and records; anti-doping agencies police fairness; broadcasters and data partners carry the game's narrative across borders. The AI-haptic era adds new stakes. Credentialing expands from eligibility to skill verification-vertical leap, serve speed, shot velocity-recorded with tamper-evident provenance. Transparency in AI-assisted methods becomes part of league integrity: what coaching aids are allowed and when, what data can be captured in competition, how injuries are monitored and reported. Transmutability ensures that when devices, models, or norms evolve, the rulebook can adapt without tearing the game's social contract.

This has obvious societal echoes. A trusted sport stack-clear rules, audited tools, portable proof-mirrors what UIS must be in higher education and workforce. The same architecture that secures a training feed can secure a learning history; the same conformance test for a helmet can inspire a conformance test for a digital credential. In both, the work is the same: align innovation with legitimacy so competition remains fair and achievement remains meaningful.

International cooperation strengthens the field. Conferences and federations can align on baseline device standards, fairness audits, and privacy protections, while letting local cultures color in the details. That is "glocal" governance again-shared spine, contextual limbs. When fans can trust that a record set in Tokyo or Knoxville means the same thing, the game's meaning compounds.

The outcome is a template: a live, beloved, high-stakes domain proving that trust is not an afterthought. It is the game plan.

We learn in the arena to contribute to our society. The arena is rehearsal for the factory, the clinic, and the classroom. Real-time feedback loops tested in sport inform industrial safety and skilled trades training; trust networks forged in competitive fairness anchor workforce credentialing; archetype collaboration under time pressure models crisis-response systems. If a varsity program can implement sensor-guided injury reduction with consent and clarity, a logistics firm can implement haptic safety cues on a warehouse floor. If a conference can govern AI video breakdowns with fairness, a college can govern AI grading aids with dignity.

The cultural transfer is as important as the technical one. Sports teach how to disagree with rules and still abide by them, how to compete fiercely without dehumanizing, how to update a meta-game without losing the soul of the game. Those are precisely the dispositions we need as we scale AI into the commons: principled iteration, public legitimacy, and care for the person behind the data point. The trust triad is the through-line: show the process, protect the vulnerable, adapt when evidence demands it.

Tennessee, Colorado, Texas, and New York are already crossing these bridges. School-based programs pair coaching analytics with AI literacy. Community colleges translate sensor feedback techniques into welding and mechatronics labs.

Employers collaborate with athletic departments on haptic and spatial computing trials before bringing them to shop floors. You can watch the diffusion pattern: fans become learners, learners become workers, workers become mentors. The arena trains a culture of improvement.

And yes, even the backyard corn hole rivalry matters: it tells you how normal people adopt tech. They try, they laugh, they nudge settings, they accept what feels helpful and reject what feels creepy. That is user research gold. If we respect that pattern, we will build tools that serve, not surveil.

The future plan for games and the like is upon us. Over the coming decade, haptics will merge with spatial computing to create fully embodied training environments; athletes will braid AI coaching with human mentorship; fans will co-create mixed-reality experiences that are part education, part celebration. The scoreboard will still tally points, but the deeper metric will be trust-between athlete and system, fan and league, human and machine. We will know we have succeeded when players say, "I feel safer and more capable," coaches say, "I see more clearly," and fans say, "I understand more deeply."

To get there, we will need coalitions that count: sport governing bodies, universities, health systems, and technology partners co-writing standards and conformance tests. We will need transparency artifacts (model cards, device safety sheets), translucence practices (layered disclosures, competition windows), and transmutability plans (firmware pipelines, rule-change protocols). We will need AwI to keep purpose ahead of performance, dignity ahead of data.

The arena will remain our proving ground. It is where we can risk change and see consequences quickly; where we can practice being faster and fairer at once. If we can steward trust here, we can export it everywhere. The game plan is simple to say and hard to do: design for excellence and equity in the same breath. That is how you win the long season.

References - Chapter 11

1. Tennessee Board of Regents (TBR). Fast Facts and System Reports 2024-2025. tbr.edu

2. Tennessee Higher Education Commission (THEC). Tennessee Higher Education Fact Book 2024-2025. tn.gov/thec

3. Tennessee Department of Labor & Workforce Development. Occupational Projections and Labor Market Information. tn.gov/workforce

4. Colorado Department of Higher Education. Credential Quality Framework; Colorado Education Exchange Pilot.highered. colorado.gov

5. Texas Higher Education Coordinating Board / Tri-Agency Workforce Initiative. Building a Talent Strong Texas; Workforce Alignment Reports. highered.texas.gov

6. State University of New York (SUNY). Microcredentials and OER Services. suny.edu

7. National Institute of Standards and Technology (NIST). AI Risk Management Framework; Trustworthy & Responsible AI Guidance. nist.gov

8. U.S. Department of Education, Office of Educational Technology. Advancing Digital Equity and AI in Learning. ed.gov

9. European Commission. Artificial Intelligence Act; European Digital Identity Wallet; Digital Decade Strategy.europa.eu; ec.europa.eu

10. UNESCO. Recommendation on the Ethics of AI; OER and Inclusion Guidance. unesco.org / unesdoc.unesco.org

11. World Health Organization (WHO). Ethics and Governance of Artificial Intelligence for Health; Equity in Digital Health Systems. who.int

12. McKinsey & Company. The State of AI in 2024; Future of Work and Skills. mckinsey.com

13. Brookings Institution. AI Governance and Equity; Trust in Digital Economies; Learning Systems. brookings.edu

14. Gartner. Trust-by-Design; Real-Time Feedback Loops; Immersive/Spatial Computing Trends. gartner.com

Chapter 12 - Social Sustainability and the AI Commons

When the arena lights dim, we step into the boardroom, the plant, the startup studio, the family shop, the open-air market. The same patterns emerge-rapid iteration, trust-governed competition, adaptive tech adoption-but now the stakes are livelihoods and social cohesion. In this chapter, the AI Commons is not just a platform; it is a marketplace, a classroom, a civic square. We must design it as a shared resource that grows prosperity and legitimacy, or it will harden divides under a polished interface.

The AI Commons makes a simple promise: anyone, anywhere, should be able to learn, verify, and apply skills with dignity. That promise requires transparent rules, translucent protections, and transmutable systems. It also requires the same archetype choreography that sports taught us to respect: Creatives to imagine new models, Builders to make them run, Laggers to temper exuberance with proof, Followers to normalize what works. The difference here is that failure is costlier. A bad call in sport loses a game; a bad call in the Commons can cost a family a livelihood.

The responsibility therefore grows with the opportunity. We must carry forward the lessons of Chapters 5-9-interoperability, learner agency, cultural relevance, real-time feedback, trustworthy verification-and weave them into business and industry without losing human texture. That is social sustainability in practice: innovation that does not burn the community it serves.

This is not an abstract plea. It is a practical operating principle: no trust, no scale; no equity, no durability.

We can move from scoreboards to scorecards - through intentional and intelligent co-design. In sport, the scoreboard is public, immediate, and legible. In business, metrics fragment-market share, supply chain velocity, employee retention, ESG performance, social license to operate. The AI Commons can bring scoreboard clarity to these scorecards if we design with the trust triad. Transparency requires plain-language reporting on outcomes that matter: not only revenue but retention, not only speed but safety, not only efficiency but equity. Translucence calibrates data sharing across partners so collaboration grows without surrendering competitive advantage or personal privacy. Transmutability ensures business models can pivot as technology and regulation evolve without breaking trust.

Consider supply chains. A "glocal" dashboard might expose carbon intensity for a German plant, spoilage risk for a Kenyan cold chain, and workforce development progress for a Tennessee facility-all in one view. The data must be auditable (transparency), shareable within roles (translucence), and updatable as standards shift (transmutability). The same pattern fits hiring, training, and safety. If a firm can show how it learns from incidents and updates controls, it earns permission to innovate. If it hides, it forfeits patience.

Colorado, Texas, and New York have begun shipping these ideas. Procurement pilots that reward transparency on labor and emissions; logistics networks that share limited-but-useful operational data; upskilling programs that publish completion and placement rates. Tennessee can press advantage by pairing UIS-verified credentials with employer scorecards, making workforce investments legible to policymakers and communities. When scorecards become shared language rather than private spreadsheets, coordination costs fall and civic trust rises. That is a compounding effect worth chasing.

Business Archetypes in the AI Commons

Creatives in the Commons are entrepreneurs, product designers, storytellers. They use AuI to discover unmet needs, sketch emergent markets, and prototype responsibly. Their workspace must be transparent enough to attract collaborators and funders, translucent enough to shield prototypes and partner secrets, and transmutable enough to pivot when the market or law shifts. The Creative's deficit is sometimes rigor; the triad supplies it by insisting on evidence and equity checks before scale.

Builders are operations leads, engineers, logistics architects. They turn concepts into systems: interoperable APIs, compliant data flows, and governance that meets both local law and global interoperability. Transparency looks like published security and performance attestations; translucence guards IP and identity; transmutability future-proofs infrastructure. Builders are judged by Tuesday morning reliability: does it work in Memphis as well as in Munich, and can it be patched overnight without drama?

Laggers-established firms and cautious investors-ask the unfashionable questions: does this pay, is it safe, who is liable? We bring them along with transparent cost-benefit cases, translucent risk previews, and transmutable integration paths that do not require total redesigns. Their gravity prevents us from scaling brittle fashions. When convinced, they add distribution and durability.

Followers-small businesses, gig workers, consumers-decide what becomes normal. They need plain-language terms of use, layered explanations of algorithmic choices, and tools that adapt across devices, bandwidths, and literacies. When Followers feel used, they churn; when they feel respected, they create the very network effects the Commons depends on. Respect is again a design choice.

The glocal model can begin anywhere, but why not begin by scaling with context and organic methodology akin to our blanket ways for engagement and interaction. "Think global, act local" is no longer a bumper sticker; it is an engineering requirement. The AI Commons must publish global layers (open data standards, ethical principles, interoperability protocols) and invite local layers (cultural, legal, economic adaptation). A supply-chain optimizer may prioritize emissions in Germany, spoilage in Kenya, and talent development in Tennessee, while still speaking a shared data language. This bifocal design is how we scale without flattening.

Transparency operates differently in each layer: global reporting for comparability, local narratives for meaning. Translucence differs too: global data-sharing agreements for backbone partners, local privacy adjustments for norms and laws. Transmutability is the hinge: global tech standards must allow region specific modules without breaking compatibility. This is the "alignment without erasure" principle we advanced in credentialing and OER.

States are proving it out. Colorado's energy sector tools travel but adapt; Texas's logistics stacks interoperate but reflect petrochemical realities; New York's finance-health tech ecosystems export patterns while honoring regulation; Tennessee's manufacturing and healthcare hubs localize global approaches to workforce and safety. Glocal design is not slower; it's smarter-and more likely to endure.

When we honor "place" while connecting across distance, we build systems people will fight for rather than fight against. That is sustainability with a spine.

Including social constructs of everyday life will embolden our findings and link them like fences to our expressed outcomes and conviction. The AI Commons will shape daily life in visible and hidden ways. Visible: personalized healthcare, adaptive education, safer transit. Hidden: credit scoring, hiring filters, dynamic pricing. For some, AI will build on-ramps-faster skill acquisition, lower barriers to entry, and a global customer base from a local storefront. For others, AI will erect walls-opaque decisions, biased datasets, exclusion from trusted networks or capital. The design test is simple: does the system make it easier for a person with less power to be recognized fairly?

AwI belongs to this junction. It asks what goals we optimize and whose costs we externalize. It insists on appeal rights, human override, and restorative pathways when harm occurs. It reminds us that consent is not a checkbox but a relationship. And it deploys the triad as a habit: transparent rules and recourse, translucent disclosures that do not overwhelm, transmutable policies that change when evidence and communities demand it.

Tennessee's lived realities-rural broadband pockets, shift-work schedules, first-generation learners-must inform interface and policy decisions. Colorado's frontier contexts, Texas's metros, New York's density present different constraints and opportunities. The Commons is sustainable only if it feels like help where people live and work.

We cannot govern by averages. We must govern by people. Perhaps there exists competition between strategy and tactic. Opportunity blossoms when AI tools are accessible across income levels; when governance ensures data fairness and algorithmic accountability; when businesses design for inclusion, not just efficiency. Entrenchment deepens when access is gated by wealth or geography, when data collection recycles historical inequities, when governance centers dominant economies and excludes emerging markets. Chapters 8 and 9 already gave us the countermeasures: real-time feedback loops that surface inequity early and trust networks that keep verification honest.

The tactical moves are plain. Subsidize or open-source essential AI tools in education and health. Require bias audits and publish results in language communities will understand. Tie public incentives to equity metrics-not as punishment, but as stewardship. Pair UIS credentials with portable rights so skills travel with the person rather than lock inside institutions. These are not moral luxuries; they are economic necessities in a tight labor market and a volatile supply chain landscape.

We should expect resistance. Transparency will surface gaps; translucence will be misread as secrecy by those who do not read nuance; transmutability will be confused with "moving the goalposts." That is where leadership matters. We narrate the why, show the data, and keep listening. Legitimacy grows from the discipline of being both firm and responsive.

Opportunity is a design choice. So is exclusion. Choose accordingly. We will design with social sustainability in mind.

A sustainable Commons rests on four pillars we can operationalize now. Credential portability: UIS-aligned, verifiable skills recognized across sectors and borders. Open access AI: public-domain algorithms for essential education and health tasks, with community auditing and local language support. Participatory governance: rule-making bodies that include archetypes-Creatives, Builders, Laggers, Followers-not as theater but as voice with vote. Adaptive economics: incentives that reward efficiency and resilience together, not one at the other's expense.

The trust triad undergirds each. Portability collapses without transparent criteria and tamper-evident verification. Open AI without translucence becomes surveillance or IP leakage. Participation without transmutability becomes museum governance-nice to look at, unfit for motion. We must design for learning systems, not legislative monuments.

Colorado's public-private councils, Texas's tri-agency mechanics, New York's public reporting norms, and Tennessee's cross-sector coalitions show muscle memory we can build upon. Each has the scars and the playbooks we need. Scale is less about new ideas and more about faithful execution.

Sustainability here is not linens and logos. It is practice, proof, and people.

I believe in self determinism and this is our culture moving from glocal commons to global stewardship. When businesses, industries, and communities align around a shared AI Commons, they practice stewardship rather than extraction. Economic health is inseparable from social cohesion; innovation without inclusion erodes legitimacy over time; global systems must remain adaptable to local needs without losing coherence. That balance is fragile and, therefore, must be designed.

Stewardship has signatures: transparent scorecards, rights and recourse for individuals, auditable standards for partners, and willingness to evolve. It also has rituals: public post-mortems when systems fail, celebratory accountability when systems work, and welcoming on-ramps for new participants. If this sounds like the culture of a great team, it should. We are building leagues of practice across industries, not simply marketplaces.

The dividend shows up in hiring, retention, vendor trust, policy patience. It shows up in fewer brittle shocks and faster recoveries. It shows up in community sentiment-the everyday indicator of whether the Commons is ours or theirs. That is not a soft metric. It is the runway for the next decade.

The work ahead is clear: keep the Commons glocal, keep the rules legible, keep the people central. If we do that, the future will not simply arrive; we will deserve it.

References - Chapters 12

1. Tennessee Board of Regents (TBR). Fast Facts and System Reports 2024-2025. tbr.edu

2. Tennessee Higher Education Commission (THEC). Tennessee Higher Education Fact Book 2024-2025. tn.gov/thec

3. Tennessee Department of Labor & Workforce Development. Occupational Projections and Labor Market Information. tn.gov/workforce

4. Colorado Department of Higher Education. Credential Quality Framework; Colorado Education Exchange Pilot.highered. colorado.gov

5. Texas Higher Education Coordinating Board / Tri-Agency Workforce Initiative. Building a Talent Strong Texas; Workforce Alignment Reports. highered.texas.gov

6. State University of New York (SUNY). Microcredentials and OER Services. suny.edu

7. National Institute of Standards and Technology (NIST). AI Risk Management Framework; Trustworthy & Responsible AI Guidance. nist.gov

8. U.S. Department of Education, Office of Educational Technology. Advancing Digital Equity and AI in Learning. ed.gov

9. European Commission. Artificial Intelligence Act; European Digital Identity Wallet; Digital Decade Strategy.europa.eu; ec.europa.eu

10. UNESCO. Recommendation on the Ethics of AI; OER and Inclusion Guidance. unesco.org / unesdoc.unesco.org

11. World Health Organization (WHO). Ethics and Governance of

Artificial Intelligence for Health; Equity in Digital Health Systems. who.int

12. McKinsey & Company. The State of AI in 2024; Future of Work and Skills. mckinsey.com

13. Brookings Institution. AI Governance and Equity; Trust in Digital Economies; Learning Systems. brookings.edu

14. Gartner. Trust-by-Design; Real-Time Feedback Loops; Immersive/Spatial Computing Trends. gartner.com

Chapter 13 - Credentialing the Future: Who Can, Who Should, and Who Will

In every era of human progress, the question of who decides has carried as much weight as what is decided. Credentialing is one of those rare decisions that defines entire generations of opportunity. For centuries, credentials have acted as social contracts-visible affirmations of skill, knowledge, and trustworthiness. A diploma on a wall, a license in a wallet, or a certification in a binder has meant more than proof of learning. It has meant recognition, legitimacy, and entry into economic and civic life.

Today, as we enter a world where humans, AI, and humanoids learn, train, and even credential side by side, the stakes grow sharper. Credentialing is no longer just about measuring what was learned in the classroom or on the job. It is about designing systems that are equitable, portable, and trusted across borders. It is about ensuring that recognition flows not only to those in elite spaces but to learners on factory floors, in rural towns, in refugee camps, and in emerging industries. It is about visibility-because what is not recognized remains invisible, and what is invisible cannot move into the economy of opportunity.

This chapter explores the enduring questions of who can credential, who should credential, and who will credential-and then examines the archetypes of credentialing, the human roles that shape, resist, and ultimately normalize new systems of recognition.

Who Can Credential?

Historically, credentialing authority rested with universities, guilds, and licensing boards. Their legitimacy was rooted in tradition and public trust. But in today's credentialing ecosystem, nearly anyone can issue a credential. Corporations mint certificates, EdTech companies issue badges, unions credential apprenticeships, and decentralized blockchain networks create "skill passports." The marketplace is flooded with credentials of varying rigor and meaning.

This expansion carries undeniable value. It democratizes recognition, allowing learning to be credentialed wherever it happens. For a machinist in rural Tennessee who learns precision welding through a community college program and then sharpens those skills through employer-led training, credentials from both experiences matter. For a veteran in Memphis using

AI-powered simulations to retrain in cybersecurity, a digital badge can signal readiness for work. For a nurse in Kenya whose credential is validated regionally and globally, the recognition enables migration and opportunity.

But the risk is credential inflation. With over one million unique credentials now available in the U.S. alone (Credential Engine, 2023), how does an employer distinguish between what is rigorous and what is ornamental? A Motlow student could hold a dozen micro-credentials, but if employers cannot discern their legitimacy, they hold little value. Without verification standards, employers hesitate, learners lose trust, and the system risks collapse.

Tennessee's statewide network of community colleges offers an antidote. By aligning credentials with Department of Labor occupational projections and embedding them in TBR-endorsed digital wallets, the state can create a filter that turns noise into clarity. Credentials would not only reflect skills but also signal economic alignment.
This ensures that every credential earned is an investment that pays off for both the learner and the workforce.

Globally, the challenge mirrors this dynamic. The European Union is advancing interoperability standards through the European Qualifications Framework (EQF), while UNESCO pushes for portable recognition of skills across borders. These efforts underscore the same point: while anyone can credential, only those embedded in trusted ecosystems will endure.

Reflection and Call to Action: Tennessee should launch a Credential Assurance Registry tied directly to THEC and TBR. Every credential, whether academic, employer-issued, or community-based, would be verified for alignment to labor market needs. This model of assurance-portable, transparent, and demand-driven-could serve as a prototype nationally and internationally.

Determining who should credential is an interesting exercise. The next question is not about capacity but about legitimacy. Who should hold the authority to credential, and under what conditions? The answer must go beyond tradition. Credentialing should rest with institutions and entities that can demonstrate rigor, fairness, and accountability. This is where the trust triad-transparency, translucence, and transmutability-becomes non-negotiable.

Transparency demands that credentialing bodies disclose evaluation rubrics and criteria. A healthcare credentialing board, for instance, must openly communicate what competencies are required for certification. Translucence requires safeguarding learner data and intellectual property while still providing enough clarity for trust.

Transmutability ensures that credentialing systems evolve as new skills-like AI ethics auditing or quantum programming-enter the workforce.

The WHO has warned that digital health systems risk inequity when credentialing does not keep pace with emerging needs. The NIST AI Risk Management Framework echoes this, reminding us that systems without adaptability quickly become irrelevant. Tennessee's simulation-driven nursing programs offer a concrete case: credentialing bodies that fail to integrate simulation outcomes risk misrepresenting the skills of new graduates.

But legitimacy is not static. It must be earned repeatedly. An accrediting body that once met rigorous standards may drift if not held accountable. This is why Tennessee's outcomes-based funding model is so important: it ties institutional legitimacy to actual learner success and workforce outcomes. Extending that principle to credentialing bodies ensures authority remains grounded in performance, not tradition.

Globally, this is echoed in UNESCO's Global Convention on the Recognition of Qualifications, which calls for transparent criteria and adaptive standards. Just as no degree should be recognized indefinitely without review, no credentialing body should retain authority without demonstrating continued fairness, adaptability, and alignment with evolving needs.

Reflection and Call to Action: Tennessee can lead by requiring five-year legitimacy reviews for all credentialing entities, modeled after accreditation cycles but tied to transparent data on outcomes and equity. Credentialing is not a one-time grant of authority; it is an ongoing covenant of trust between institutions and the people they serve.

If we do nothing, credentialing authority will consolidate in the hands of those with the deepest resources-global technology companies. Their scale, speed, and innovation are unmatched, but their incentives may not align with public good.

Imagine a future where credentials are controlled by a handful of platforms, accessible only to those who can pay, transferable only within their ecosystems. This is not equity-it is monopoly. However, what would be the prerequisites to have individuals or other entities certified as credentialing agents adjacent to trusted organizations?

The alternative is deliberate coalition-building. Governments bring regulatory oversight. Universities offer academic rigor. Employers bring real-world alignment. Civil society organizations ensure equity and inclusivity. Together, they balance one another. This is already happening: Colorado's Credential Exchange aligns education and labor data. Texas's Tri-Agency Workforce Initiative connects education, labor, and economic development. SUNY in New York has harmonized micro-credentials across one of the largest systems in the country.

Tennessee, too, has begun experimenting with statewide initiatives, aligning higher education outcomes with labor force needs through TBR and THEC. But to go further, the state must institutionalize a Credentialing Council-a coalition of higher education leaders, employers, policymakers, and learners that meets regularly to update standards, publish public dashboards, and ensure adaptability.

Globally, we can see models of such coalitions taking shape. The African Union is considering continent-wide credentialing frameworks to support mobility. The EU has moved toward shared recognition through the EQF. The U.S. risks lagging behind if it does not design national coalitions of its own.

Reflection and Call to Action: The future of credentialing must not be monopolized. It must be shared. Tennessee should create a Credentialing Council for Equity and Growth, balancing authority across academia, industry, government, and civil society. Only coalitions can prevent credentialing from becoming another vector of inequality.

The Archetypes in Credentialing

Credentialing is not only about systems-it is about people. The adoption, legitimacy, and scalability of credentialing ecosystems are shaped by archetypes: the Creatives, the Builders, the Laggers, the Followers, and now, the Collectors. Together, they form a dynamic matrix that ensures systems are not dominated by a single worldview but evolve through diverse engagement.

The Creatives

Creatives are visionaries. They imagine modular formats like micro-credentials, skill passports, or blockchain-secured wallets that recognize both formal and informal learning. At Motlow, a Creative might propose a credentialing system that validates both classroom learning and community service, making visible what was once invisible. Globally, a Creative might push for a skills passport portable across borders.

But creativity without grounding risks becoming untethered. A badge designed without employer input may look impressive but carry little market value. A blockchain wallet may be technically brilliant but ignored if it lacks interoperability. Creatives thrive when paired with Builders, who can translate vision into usable systems.

Creatives embody the transmutability of the trust triad. Their role is to push systems beyond the present, envisioning futures that can adapt as new data, technologies, and needs emerge. Without them, credentialing stagnates. With them, credentialing evolves.

At their best, Creatives ensure credentialing captures the full humanity of learning-formal, informal, academic, vocational, and lived. But they need discipline. Without checks, they risk creating systems that are inspiring but impractical. Their task is to balance imagination with grounding, ensuring vision translates into reality.

The Builders

Builders are implementers. They take ideas and forge them into systems. At the state level, Builders might design platforms linking TBR-issued micro-credentials with Tennessee Department of Labor projections, ensuring credentials are both portable and relevant. At the global level, Builders create interoperable standards that allow credentials to move seamlessly across borders.

Yet Builders risk rigidity. If they over-standardize, they may stifle innovation. If they under-standardize, they may fail to create trust. Builders thrive when they embrace transparency in development cycles-making criteria, testing, and performance visible to all stakeholders.

Without Builders, ideas remain vapor. With Builders, credentialing systems become infrastructure. Their work ensures scale, durability, and trust. But Builders must also remain adaptable. Systems engineered too rigidly become brittle, unable to respond to changing needs. Builders must therefore design for transmutability, embedding flexibility into their systems.

Globally, Builders include the engineers of the EQF, the architects of the Texas

Tri-Agency framework, and the coders of blockchain credentialing platforms. Locally, they are the staff at Motlow or TBR ensuring micro-credentials integrate with employer demand data. Builders sit at the fulcrum of vision and execution.

The Laggers

Laggers wait. They adopt late, preferring to see systems prove themselves in the real world. In Tennessee, this may be an employer who refuses to recognize micro-credentials until several cohorts demonstrate clear outcomes. In global contexts, it may be governments reluctant to align with blockchain-based registries until fraud-prevention measures are validated.

Though often criticized, Laggers serve an essential role. They test legitimacy. If a credential cannot withstand their skepticism, it is not robust. Laggers embody the transparency principle of the trust triad, demanding visible proof before adoption. Their caution keeps systems honest.

Laggers may frustrate innovators, but they are invaluable validators. Their resistance highlights weak points and forces systems to prove themselves in the messy realities of workplaces and communities. In a way, Laggers are credentialing's stress testers.

By incorporating Laggers into the ecosystem, we ensure that credentialing systems are robust enough to withstand skepticism. They do not prevent innovation; they temper it. Their cautious validation ensures systems work not only in theory but also in practice.

The Followers

Followers normalize systems once trust is established. They are the students, employees, and citizens who adopt credentials at scale. A learner may initially resist digital wallets, but once they see peers hired faster because of verified credentials, they embrace it. A small business in Murfreesboro may begin accepting state-issued micro-credentials once larger firms normalize them.

Followers matter because they scale systems into norms. They embody the translucence of the trust triad-they do not need full technical knowledge of how systems work, but they must see enough to trust them. Their feedback shapes refinements and ensures systems remain human-centered.

Once Followers adopt, credentialing systems move from experiment to expectation. Their collective participation shifts systems from the margins into the mainstream.

Without them, no credential can gain cultural traction.

In essence, Followers make credentialing real. They may not design or build, but they validate by living within the system. Their lived experience is the final measure of whether credentialing delivers on its promises of mobility, equity, and opportunity.

The Collectors

Collectors are a new archetype in credentialing. They thrive on accumulation-gathering micro-credentials, digital badges, certificates, and recognitions across diverse fields. A student might stack dozens of badges through online platforms, or a professional may pursue endless micro-credentials to remain competitive. Collectors are motivated by curiosity, ambition, and sometimes anxiety in a rapidly shifting economy.

Collectors can drive innovation by showing how credentials stack and intersect. A Tennessee student might combine mechatronics, coding, and communication badges to carve a unique skill profile attractive to advanced manufacturing firms. But Collectors also expose risks. Without alignment, they may accumulate credentials with little coherence or labor market value. Employers may struggle to interpret their sprawling portfolios.

The challenge with Collectors is translation. Systems must help employers and institutions make sense of collections, filtering noise into meaningful signals. Collectors embody the entire trust triad: transparency to display what was earned, translucence to protect sensitive learning data, and transmutability to update collections as skills evolve. Properly supported, Collectors become lifelong learners and workforce innovators. Left unsupported, they risk credential fatigue and disillusionment.

Globally, Collectors mirror the ethos of lifelong learning called for by UNESCO and the OECD. Locally, they represent the future of Tennessee's workforce, where adaptability and continuous learning are paramount. Collectors remind us that the future of credentialing is not linear-it is cumulative, layered, and dynamic.

The Glocal Credentialing Model

Every conversation on credentialing eventually arrives at the tension between the global and the local. How do we design a system that is globally portable but locally grounded? How do we balance the shared need for consistency with the equally pressing need for cultural, legal, and economic specificity? This is the essence of the glocal credentialing model: globally trusted, locally adaptable, and layered in its validation.

In Tennessee, this challenge is clear. A micro-credential in advanced manufacturing should align with global standards of robotics and automation, ensuring portability to Germany or Japan. But it must also reflect the specific equipment and safety codes used at Nissan's Smyrna plant or Ultium's Spring Hill facility. Similarly, a nursing credential in Tennessee must meet WHO standards for global portability but also satisfy the Tennessee Board of Nursing's unique requirements. The global cannot erase the local; the local cannot ignore the global.

Globally, we see this balance in practice. Kenya's nursing credentials are now being validated for migration programs through WHO-aligned competency frameworks. In Europe, the EQF ensures that credentials earned in Italy are recognized in Germany, even as each country retains local control. In the U.S., SUNY's micro-credentialing framework provides coherence across a massive system, while local campuses still tailor offerings to regional labor needs.

Layered systems provide the way forward. Credentials must be stackable and verifiable at multiple levels: local (recognized by regional employers), state (validated by workforce boards), national (aligned to Department of Labor projections), and international (benchmarked to global frameworks). A machinist in Tennessee might train with humanoid-assisted instruction, earn a credential through Motlow, and then present it on the global stage, where it is recognized instantly by employers in Munich or Singapore.

But the risk of glocal models is unevenness. If too much weight is placed on global portability, local nuances may be erased. If too much emphasis is placed on local specificity, credentials may lose global legitimacy. This balance must be designed into the system intentionally, not left to chance.

Reflection and Call to Action: Tennessee can pilot a glocal credential wallet that layers validation-local to global-on every credential. Imagine a student in Murfreesboro holding a welding badge that is simultaneously recognized by a local union, validated by the state's workforce board, mapped to federal labor codes, and benchmarked globally to ISO standards. This layering transforms a credential from a static document into a living passport of skills.

Risks of Credentialing in the New Age

Every opportunity carries risk. In credentialing, the risks are stark: entrenchment, opacity, and lock-in. Without inclusive governance, credentials risk becoming yet another gatekeeping tool, reinforcing inequities instead of dismantling them.
Entrenchment occurs when access to credentials is gated by wealth, geography, or privilege. In Tennessee, a rural student without broadband may be unable to access the same digital credentials as a peer in Nashville. Globally, learners in low-income countries risk exclusion if credentialing platforms require costly subscriptions. Equity must be designed in, not assumed.

Opacity is equally dangerous. An AI-driven credential that cannot explain its scoring is a credential without accountability. Employers may hesitate to trust it; learners may resent it. The NIST AI Risk Management Framework warns of "black box credentialing"-systems that certify without explanation. Transparency must remain the bedrock.

Lock-in is perhaps the most insidious risk. Proprietary credential systems that cannot transfer between employers, states, or countries create monopolies. Imagine if a credential earned in Tennessee could only be verified within one platform, leaving learners trapped. This is already happening with certain corporate training certifications. Once locked in, learners have no mobility, and employers have no interoperability.

The alternative is intentional design. With transparency, equity, and interoperability built into systems, risks transform into opportunities. Opportunity means credentials that travel with the person, not the platform. Equity means informal and lived learning is recognized alongside formal systems. Mobility means that a single credential can unlock doors locally, nationally, and globally.

Reflection and Call to Action: Tennessee must publish an annual credential risk audit, identifying risks of entrenchment, opacity, and lock-in across all credentialing entities. By naming risks publicly, we create accountability-and accountability is the first guardrail against inequity.

Trust Networks as Credentialing Ecosystems

Here we arrive at the heart of the matter: trust. Credentialing without trust is theater. It may look official, but it carries no weight. Trust transforms credentials into currency. But what happens when there is distrust? What occurs when networks are revealed to be untrustworthy, opaque, or manipulated? Do we move toward civil discourse or civil discord?

We cannot assume trust will be permanent. Even in high-trust networks, breaches occur. A hacked registry, a fraudulent issuer, or a biased AI credentialing tool can erode confidence overnight. In Tennessee, one compromised digital wallet could jeopardize the legitimacy of an entire system. Globally, a breach in one node of the EU's EQF could ripple across dozens of countries. Trust is fragile; distrust is contagious.

Responding to distrust requires resilience. Systems must have redundancy-so one compromised node does not bring down the whole. They must have rapid incident response, so breaches are acknowledged and addressed transparently. They must have continuous audits, ensuring weaknesses are identified before they are exploited. Most importantly, they must invite civil discourse-acknowledging distrust openly rather than ignoring it. If not, distrust metastasizes into discord, where systems fracture and legitimacy is lost. The trust triad-transparency, translucence, and transmutability-becomes the antidote to distrust. Transparency ensures breaches are visible and addressed publicly. Translucence protects sensitive data even during crises, preserving confidence. Transmutability ensures that credentialing frameworks evolve, patching vulnerabilities without collapsing entirely.

Globally, we can learn from anti-doping systems in sports, which maintain trust through relentless transparency, independent audits, and global cooperation. Locally, Tennessee can adopt similar principles: open credential registries, independent validation nodes, and rapid public accountability for breaches. Trust is not a given-it is cultivated, maintained, and, when broken, rebuilt with humility.

Reflection and Call to Action: Tennessee should anchor credentialing in a Trust by Design Charter, committing every entity to transparency, redundancy, and public accountability. When trust is tested-and it will be-the measure of our system will not be whether distrust emerges but how we respond.

Credentialing as a Peace and Growth Mechanism

Credentialing is not just about jobs. It is about stability. In fragile economies or conflict zones, credentials provide a lifeline. A refugee arriving in Tennessee with a verifiable credential can work immediately, bypassing bureaucratic delays. In disaster recovery, portable credentials accelerate rebuilding by mobilizing skilled labor quickly. In emerging economies, AI-verified credentials bypass corruption, ensuring recognition is based on skills, not bribes.

This is not theoretical. The World Bank and UNESCO have already documented the power of portable credentials in enabling displaced persons to integrate into new economies. The WHO has called for global health credentials to address shortages in elder care. Tennessee's own workforce initiatives show the same principle: credentials aligned with employer demand can stabilize families, communities, and regions.

But credentials as peace mechanisms face obstacles. If they are inaccessible, biased, or exclusionary, they exacerbate instability. If they are monopolized, they breed resentment. If they lack portability, they trap people in cycles of poverty. The stakes are high: credentialing can either reduce tension or inflame it.

Humanoids add another layer. A humanoid in a refugee camp could both train and verify skills in real time, accelerating integration. Hybrid credentialing teams-human, AI, humanoid-could validate competencies in hazardous environments. This is not about replacing human dignity but about extending recognition into spaces where human capacity is stretched.

The economic growth dimension is equally vital. Tennessee's manufacturing sector demonstrates how portable credentials accelerate hiring. Globally, the OECD projects that economies with transparent credentialing systems will experience faster workforce integration and lower unemployment. Credentialing is not peripheral to economic growth-it is its foundation.

Reflection and Call to Action: Tennessee should lead in piloting a Peace and Growth Credential Framework, designed for both local resilience and global portability. By aligning with WHO, UNESCO, and OECD standards, while grounding in TBR and THEC data, Tennessee can model how credentialing stabilizes both economies and communities. In this way, credentialing becomes more than recognition-it becomes resilience itself.

References - Chapter 13

1. Credential Engine. Counting Credentials 2023. credentialengine.org

2. UNESCO. Global Convention on the Recognition of Qualifications; Ethics of AI. unesco.org

3. OECD. Skills for Jobs; Future of Skills and Credentials. oecd.org

4. WHO. Digital Health and Equity; Ethics and Governance of AI in Health. who.int

5. NIST. AI Risk Management Framework. nist.gov

6. World Bank. World Development Report: Education and Skills. worldbank.org

7. Education Design Lab. Skills and Micro-pathways. eddesignlab.org

8. SUNY. Microcredentials Framework. suny.edu

9. Tennessee Board of Regents (TBR). Outcomes-Based Funding and Workforce Data. tbr.edu

10. Tennessee Higher Education Commission (THEC). Fact Book; Labor and Outcomes Reports. tn.gov/thec

11. Tennessee Department of Labor. Occupational Projections. tn.gov/workforce

12. Texas Higher Education Coordinating Board. Tri-Agency Workforce Initiative. highered.texas.gov

13. Colorado Department of Higher Education. Credential Quality Framework. highered.colorado.gov

Epilogue

Enduring in Front: Stewardship Beyond the Algorithm

If the prologue was a call to step out in front, then the epilogue is a charge to endure in that position-to continue walking forward when the terrain shifts, when the lights dim, and when the easy option is to retreat. Leadership is not a sprint to a single summit; it is a long ascent through shifting weather, requiring resolve, humility, and a steady hand. To endure is to accept that visibility brings responsibility, and that responsibility is sustained not by applause but by conviction.

Beyond the algorithm lies a greater truth: technology is only as transformative as the human spirit that wields it. Artificial intelligence, policy frameworks, digital ecosystems, and governance models are instruments, not destinations. They amplify our capacity to learn, earn, and own, but they also remind us of our duty to steward those capacities wisely. We must be as deliberate in cultivating moral imagination as we are in writing code or crafting legislation. What matters most is not whether AI can predict a choice, but whether leaders can preserve freedom, dignity, and possibility in the choices that remain.

Enduring in front requires clarity about purpose and a willingness to stay present when complexity threatens to overwhelm. It is the ability to resist the seduction of easy metrics, to look beyond dashboards and profit margins to the subtler indicators of trust, equity, and belonging. It is the discipline to embed governance into innovation, to ensure that speed does not eclipse safety, and that efficiency does not erode empathy. It is the vigilance to remember that algorithms are authored, and that authorship carries an ethical weight that cannot be automated away.

As we step back and consider the closing arc of this work, we see how the themes of Volume II converge to shape stewardship in practice. In sports, we saw how feedback loops refine performance-how iterative learning transforms raw potential into precision, how honest data, applied wisely, can elevate a team beyond talent into collective excellence. In business, we saw how the glocal model balances scale with context-how leaders must stretch between global reach and local roots, honoring the specific while sustaining the whole. In humanoids, we saw the care mandate and the potential for peace, a reminder that even in silicon and alloy, our most enduring technologies must serve compassion before conquest.

And now, in credentialing, we encounter the keystone: recognition. Because if skills, knowledge, and contributions remain invisible, they are functionally nonexistent in the marketplace of opportunity. Credentialing in the AI age is not merely about measuring what is - it is about making visible what is possible. It is about ensuring that learning, whether born in classrooms, on factory floors, within communities, or in digital spaces, is affirmed and valued. To credential wisely is to extend dignity to effort, to cast light on potential, to knit opportunity into the fabric of trust.

Leading while doing demands endurance-not the endurance of survival alone, but the endurance of success, of impact, of vision that lasts. It is the endurance of building systems of trust in a world that often prefers convenience to conscience. It is the endurance of teaching, innovating, learning, and training when the headlines shift and the funding cycles turn. It is the endurance of remaining deeply human in the midst of machine speed: slowing down enough to see the people behind the data, the stories behind the signals, the futures embedded in every decision.

To be out in front is to carry both burden and blessing. To endure in front is to accept that our role as leaders is never to finish the work, but to ensure the work endures beyond us-sustainable, ethical, and expansive enough to hold generations yet to come. We plant seeds whose shade we may never sit beneath, yet we plant them because leadership is a covenant with time, not a transaction with the present.

The algorithm will continue to evolve. Policies will be rewritten. Governance will adapt. Yet the call to steward wisely will not expire. Our task remains constant: to lead with courage, to do with integrity, to keep faith with the communities we serve, and to ensure that those who follow inherit not just systems, but possibilities-possibilities spacious enough for creativity, equity, and hope.

The last chapter of *A Transformative Future with AI* hopefully left those who read the volume grounded in policy formation, equity & access, emerging tech integration, and the metaphor of "planting a tree for which we may never sit under." What follows was not to reset, but to acknowledge what has been formed and pick-up mid stride. We have built the scaffolding; now the world is climbing upon it. It is not what can AI do, but how we must embody our stewardship of the "how's and why's" of responsibility at scale. This is not the end. This is the final cadence of holding space, or creating it while forging a basis of continuity to keep our systems thinking voices intact. It is a continuation - a reminder that stewardship is not about final words, but about lasting actions. The best part of the process is still ahead. In my humble opinion, the dark early mornings, the collation of notes, scrap paper, and the middle of the night voice notes (so we don't forget in the morning) … the WORK! Out in front, still, we endure: navigating uncertainty with anchored purpose, balancing progress with protection, daring to imagine futures where humanity and technology walk forward together, resilient and unafraid.

www.ingramcontent.com/pod-product-compliance
Lightning Source LLC
LaVergne TN
LVHW070855210926
848482LV00016B/938